A Taste of Mustique

A Taste of Mustique

Kevin Snook
With Elizabeth Penniman
Photography by **Sophie Munro**
With a foreword by **Mick Jagger**

MACMILLAN
CARIBBEAN

Macmillan Education
Between Towns Road, Oxford, OX4 3PP
A division of Macmillan Publishers Limited
Companies and representatives throughout the world

www.macmillan-caribbean.com

ISBN: 978-1-4050-9906-6

Design by Joe Hodanich
Cover design by Joe Hodanich, Evolve Creative, and Sophie Munro
Cover photographs by Sophie Munro

Printed and bound in Thailand

2011 2010 2009 2008 2007
10 9 8 7 6 5 4 3 2

This book is dedicated to my Wonderful Boys – Christopher, Daniel, and Elliot. Wishing them only the best as they take their Life's Journey.

I love you with all my heart,
Dad xxx

and

With a special tribute to all the Vincentian people with whom I've had the pleasure of working. . .Thank you for making my time here so enjoyable, and for teaching me your wonderful ways.

Respect,
Kevin Snook

To the memory of my father, Russell Penniman, and to his wife, Lorie, who gave the beauty of Mustique to my heart. . .
for me to share with my incredible children –
Caroline, Russell, and William

My Love Always,
Elizabeth Penniman

Contents

Foreword

THE BEAUTY OF MUSTIQUE – AND THE ROLE WE ALL PLAY IN ITS PRESERVATION

There are many small islands throughout the world that people have attempted to develop, but not always with the interests of the environment in mind. Since its inception in 1968, the Mustique Company has recognized both the aesthetic and economic value of a healthy environment and has tried to protect the island from ad hoc and adverse development. This was accomplished by partitioning the island into a limited number of plots, having the island and surrounding waters to one kilometer offshore declared a Conservation Area, and commissioning studies and reports to monitor environmental issues and concerns as they arose. The result of this is an island that is still mostly covered with green space – nearly 70 percent – with a diverse collection of plant communities, habitats, and the creatures that depend upon these. The dominant categories of vegetation on Mustique remain unchanged, these being the sheltered forests and the windswept forests alike.

The Company recognizes that all parts of a small island's ecosystem are interrelated and therefore all are important to maintain a healthy environment. The sea salt ponds are not only important for bird life, they also provide a sink for the soil that runs down the hillside during heavy rains. This in turn helps prevent runoff of silt from entering the sea and covering our sea grass beds and coral reefs. The coral reefs not only provide food and shelter for fish and other creatures, they also protect our white sandy beaches from storm waves.

The Development Plan created for Mustique is a testament to the Company's desire to maintain its valuable natural resources while allowing limited development in carefully selected areas.

The goal of environmental management on Mustique is to preserve and use all facets of the environment in such a manner that they will remain in perpetuity for future generations.

Mick Jagger

Preface

There are places in our world that stimulate and awaken senses we never knew existed. The island of Mustique is just such a place.

Every day on this magical, small jewel of land, the island morning arrives with a glorious sun coming up over the clearest ocean blue waters to awaken every heart. The kitchens of Mustique bring us hot, bubbling coffee, thinly sliced glistening local fruits, steaming fantastical soups, and clean and simple seafood to awaken our souls.

Mustique has a flavor unlike any other. Mustique has a taste unlike any other. Mustique is an island unlike any other. Your taste buds will know you have arrived long before your body has realized the transformation: it starts with the subtlety of the salty breeze and is nurtured with the first sip of rummy nectar-like punch; it is complete when you fall asleep with the taste of the island still on your tongue.

Mustique has a rhythm. Over breakfast, listen to the syncopation of the small planes coming and going every few minutes, waves quietly tapping at sandy beaches, birds gossiping, and turtles rustling through the grasses. A person lucky enough to spend time on Mustique will quickly realize that their pulse inevitably and seamlessly joins the magical island tempo.

Mustique has a spirit. As you enjoy lunch on the beach or around a large table filled with friends old and new, notice the harmony of smiling children, gracious hosts, laughing fishermen, and tender guardians. A person lucky enough to know Mustique will always carry a grain of the island soul in their heart.

Mustique has a vibrancy. Over dinner, observe the palette of painted silks, a beautiful sun setting over translucent azure waters, fruits more colorful than the stars, and flowers playing hide-and-seek. A person lucky enough to be enveloped in this vivid island quilt will hum with melodic content.

As the day finishes with sweet island delicacies under the Caribbean moon, in a quiet corner of a quiet island home at the end of a quiet dirt road, there is a painting hanging gently on the wall in an outside breezeway. The painting is beautiful, to be certain, but the wonder of this peaceful scene is not in the brush strokes or the subtlety of hues or the image of a loving embrace. The wonder of this scene is perched above the painting on two short inches of the stretched canvas frame; content to watch the breezes blowing through the trees beyond, a hummingbird sits in her nest and looks out over her Mustique. She is satisfied just feeling the island around her. She is at ease as the warm breeze gently touches her feathers. This tropical tranquility is in every tiny bone of her opalescent form.

Some cultures believe the hummingbird is actually the sun in disguise. Once you've stepped foot on Mustique, it's easy to see why the sun would consider this island her home.

Here, we have brought a sampling of recipes from the island of Mustique to take with you – wherever that may be. We have found some island favorites and standards, added a few others which incorporate the unique and special flavors of the Caribbean, and tapped into the files of some the island's best chefs and residents to bring the "Taste of Mustique" home for every reader.

We are also proud that a portion of the proceeds from the sales of *A Taste of Mustique* will go to support the Environmental Committee of Mustique Island, directed by the Mustique Board of Directors – to ensure that the silent beauty of the hummingbirds, the slow trek of the tortoises, the perfume of the flowers and trees, and the pristine and perfect beaches these creatures call home will be here, unspoiled, for many years to come.

Elizabeth Penniman

Introduction

My idea for this book

arrived three years ago during a rainy afternoon at Basil's Bar, while contemplating life. I wanted to portray Mustique in a different way than had been published before, something other than a focus on our island's famous homeowners and their villas. I decided to take a trip into the culinary aspects of these Grenadine Islands, focusing on Mustique and presenting the story of the working people that make this island tick.

I've been privileged to have cooked and taught in many of Mustique's homes, where the local cooks welcomed me with open arms and passed on their knowledge of their Caribbean ingredients and their cooking techniques, which have evolved and become part of my own cooking style. I love to teach, but I've also prepared and organized many catered affairs, from intimate dinner parties to beachside barbecues and themed cocktail parties . . . It has all been so memorable, always interesting, and a real gift.

Caribbean food is influenced by many cultures, to include Africa, Asia, Europe, and the Americas, and it is surprising to me that this cuisine has yet to come to the forefront of popular culinary culture, rich as it is with its diversity, flavor, and the use of fresh local ingredients.

My approach and philosophy to food is really quite simple: fresh, seasonal, and uncomplicated ideas and presentations in a world where our lives sometimes aren't as simple. I welcome you into my kitchen, and hope you find inspiration and a wave of island memories from the pages of this book.

Kevin Snook
Mustique

Mustique Morning Glory

CHAPTER ONE

Mustique Morning Glory: A Sunshine Breakfast

A feast of sunlight. Sunrise for the early birds is a favorite time of the new day …a time of real peace and solitude before the island awakens. The songs of the tree frogs have long been silent, and with the early morning sun we hear birdsong, ocean waves,

and turtles making their way out from under the bougainvillea to find their own morning fare. We consider breakfast to be the most important and refreshing meal…to create our energy and spirit for the Mustique day …whatever it may bring.

Recipes

Papaya yogurt nectar | Mango morning nectar | Honey-roasted granola with fresh mangoes and Vincentian yogurt

Banana cinnamon muffins | Morning glory muffins | Ginger waffles with fresh mango preserve

Cinnamon raisin French toast with seasonal fruits | Spiced pancakes with chunky pineapple sauce and toasted pecans

Potato and sweet potato cakes with crispy bacon | Sorrel drink

Papaya yogurt nectar

INGREDIENTS
1¹/₃ cups plain yogurt
3 cups peeled and cubed ripe papaya
½ cup freshly squeezed orange juice
3 tsp honey
4 cups low-fat milk
chilled lime slices, to garnish

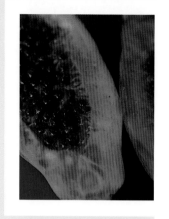

PREPARATION
Blend all ingredients together in a food processor until smooth. Serve in tall chilled glasses, garnished, if desired, with a chilled lime slice on the rim of each glass.

Serves 6

Loaded with vitamins, and sometimes called pawpaw or "the banana of the tropics," papaya is a wonderful fruit, best combined with a more distinct flavor to bring out its wonderful, subtly rich taste.

Mango morning nectar

INGREDIENTS
2 cups peeled and cubed ripe mango
2 tbsp sugar
3 tbsp freshly squeezed lime juice
4 cups soda water

PREPARATION
Blend all ingredients together in a food processor until smooth, and serve in tall glasses.

Serves 6

Known as the fruit of the tropics, mangoes can be found nearly everywhere year-round to bring this tropical taste home.

Honey-roasted granola with fresh mangoes and Vincentian yogurt

Serves 6

A wonderful wholesome and healthy start to the day, providing a great source of energy with a fabulous combination of easy-to-find ingredients.

INGREDIENTS
2 tbsp raisins
2 tbsp currants
2 tbsp dried banana slices
2 tbsp dates
2 tbsp prunes
2 tbsp dried apricot pieces
2 tbsp dried pineapple pieces
½ cup rolled oats
½ cup oat bran
¼ cup sweetened flaked coconut
¼ cup slivered almonds
¼ cup sunflower seeds
1 cup honey
plain yogurt and fresh mango slices, to serve

PREPARATION
Preheat oven to 350°F.

Mix all the fruit ingredients together, and add the honey. Stir well. Spread out on a baking sheet and roast for 15–20 minutes, stirring a few times while baking.

Allow to cool, and add to the remaining dry ingredients.

This is also good made with maple syrup instead of honey. It will keep well in a sealed container. Serve with plain yogurt and fresh mango slices.

Banana cinnamon muffins

INGREDIENTS

1 cup bran

¼ cup milk

1½ cups mashed, ripe banana

1¼ cups unbleached white flour

¼ cup brown sugar

1 tsp baking soda

1 tsp baking powder

¼ tsp sea salt

1 tsp ground cinnamon

½ cup chopped dates

2 large eggs

4 tbsp melted butter

1 tsp vanilla extract

PREPARATION

Preheat oven to 350°F.

Combine the bran, milk, and banana and let rest for 5 minutes.

In a separate bowl, mix together the flour, sugar, soda, baking powder, sea salt, cinnamon, and dates. Add to the banana mixture.

Beat together the eggs, butter, and vanilla and combine with the banana mixture. **Do not over mix.**

Spoon into a well-greased muffin pan, and bake for 15 minutes.

Makes 8 large muffins

There always seems to be an abundance of bananas on our island, which combine with cinnamon in a perfect union to start the new day.

Morning glory muffins

Makes 8 large muffins

This hearty and healthy eclectic mix of ingredients creates an interesting and wonderful taste with every bite. Crunchy, soft, moist, yum!

INGREDIENTS

1 cup all-purpose flour

½ cup white sugar

1 tsp baking soda

1 tsp ground cinnamon

¼ tsp sea salt

¼ cup grated carrot

1 small apple, peeled, cored and grated

¼ cup diced pineapple

¼ cup raisins

¼ cup chopped pecans

¼ cup sweetened flaked coconut

2 eggs

¼ cup melted unsalted butter

1 tsp vanilla extract

PREPARATION

Preheat oven to 350°F.

In a large bowl, mix together the flour, sugar, baking soda, cinnamon, and sea salt. Stir in the grated carrot, apple, pineapple, raisins, nuts, and coconut.

In a separate bowl, beat together the eggs, butter, and vanilla. Mix into the flour until the batter is just combined. Spoon into a well-greased muffin pan, and bake for 20 minutes.

Serve warm, spread with unsalted butter.

Ginger waffles with fresh mango preserve

INGREDIENTS

Waffles:
2 cups unbleached sifted white flour
2½ tsp baking powder
½ tsp baking soda
½ tsp sea salt
1½ tbsp brown sugar
1 tbsp powdered ginger
½ tsp ground cinnamon
4 eggs, separated
1 cup plain yogurt
1½ cups milk
¾ cup melted unsalted butter
powdered sugar, to serve

Mango preserve:
4 tbsp melted butter
2 tbsp brown sugar
1 tsp lemon juice
2 tbsp water
4 ripe mangoes, peeled, stoned and coarsely chopped

PREPARATION

Combine the flour, baking powder, baking soda, sea salt, sugar, ginger, and cinnamon in a bowl.

In a separate bowl, whisk together the egg yolks, yogurt, milk, and melted butter. Add to the flour mixture and stir thoroughly. Beat the egg whites until stiff, and gently fold into the mixture.

Pour the waffle mixture onto a waffle iron according to the manufacturer's instructions.

For the mango preserve, put the melted butter into a stainless-steel pan on a low heat. Add the sugar, lemon juice, water, and mangoes. Slowly simmer until the fruit is soft. Spoon over the finished waffles and serve with a dusting of powdered sugar.

The mango preserve may be made a day ahead and reheated.

Makes 8 waffles

The subtlety of our island ginger spice makes for a comforting breakfast dish, with a wonderful aroma and sweet rich flavor.

A Man Walks into a Bar

One day at sunset, a customer sitting at the Firefly bar asked to sign his bill. Not recognizing him, Firefly's celebrated bartender, Patrick, asked the man where he was staying, to which the reply was "Obsidian" – Lord Litchfield's villa. According to the Mustique Island arrivals list, another family was staying there who were well known to us, so I was asked to question the customer. I told him that we were a bit confused, and he explained that the scheduled guests had cancelled due to illness, and he had taken their place. As he seemed to know what he was talking about, I decided all was fine and asked him to sign the tab and print his name. He replied that his name was Pierce Brosnan and I said (not recognizing him either), "Fine, just sign and print your name." He looked at me sideways, winked, and said his name again, adding, "As in James Bond…!" I then realized who he was and said, "You can't be, you look nothing like Sean Connery!" Fortunately he found this amusing, and returned that evening with his family … and now we look forward to seeing him every year.

Stan Clayton

Cinnamon raisin French toast with seasonal fruits

INGREDIENTS
4 eggs

¼ cup milk

¼ cup cream

2 tbsp brown sugar

pinch of sea salt

2 tbsp dark rum

¼ tsp ground cinnamon

2 tbsp melted butter

2 tbsp canola oil

6 thick slices of fresh raisin bread

seasonal fruits and grated nutmeg or maple syrup, to serve

PREPARATION
Mix together the eggs, milk, cream, sugar, sea salt, rum, and cinnamon in a bowl to form a batter.

On medium heat, pour some of the butter and oil into a non-stick pan or iron skillet.

Dip each slice of raisin bread as needed into the batter and allow to soak slightly. Lift out of batter and fry until brown on both sides. Repeat with each slice of bread, adding more butter and oil to the pan as necessary.

To serve, cut each slice into triangles and arrange on plates with seasonal fruits. Sprinkle with grated nutmeg or drizzle with warm maple syrup.

Serves 3–4

This is a classic breakfast, with a hint of rum and fruits at their prime . . .

Breakfast on Mustique

Ghost koi, their sunflower-yellow button eyes
Unstitched, weave shadow in the morning sun
And suck on moss-backed stones. The tree ants run
In patrols, their only thought to tyrannize
Some hapless aphid. Scab-red dragon-flies
Patrol just out of reach, jaws set to stun
Their careless prey and drain them, one by one.
Night lilies fold away amidst the cries
Of bequia-sweets at table, sword-sharp beaks
Extended – each scrap of food defended
From its neighbor. A tortoise heaves and wins
First prize: hibiscus flowers! Our kitten sneaks
Some bacon. The hungry night has ended;
Another day in Paradise begins.

Felix Dennis
Mustique

Ghost koi are a pure silver-white variety of ornamental fish. The Japanese call them
hikarimono or ogon. Bequia-sweets (Quiscalus lugubris) are a form of Carib grackle, common
throughout the Lesser Antilles. Sharp-eyed, bold and abusive, they squabble interminably.
Bequia, an island close by Mustique, is pronounced "beckway."

Spiced pancakes with chunky pineapple sauce and toasted pecans

Serves 6

INGREDIENTS

Pineapple sauce:

2 ripe pineapples, peeled, cored and coarsely chopped

½ cup pineapple juice

½ cup corn syrup

2 tbsp lemon juice

1 cup toasted pecans

Pancakes:

1½ cups all-purpose flour

¼ tsp sea salt

¼ cup brown sugar

1 tsp baking powder

1 tsp baking soda

$1/3$ tsp ground cinnamon

$1/3$ tsp grated nutmeg

$1/3$ tsp powdered ginger

1½ cups milk

2 tbsp molasses

2 tbsp melted butter

4 egg whites, lightly beaten

oil for greasing

PREPARATION

For the pineapple sauce, place all the ingredients in a stainless-steel pot on medium to low heat, and cook slowly for about 30 minutes. Adjust the sweetness, if desired.

In a medium-sized bowl, sift together the flour, sea salt, brown sugar, baking powder, baking soda, cinnamon, nutmeg, and ginger. In a separate bowl, combine the milk, molasses, and melted butter with the egg whites. Add the flour mixture and stir until just blended – **do not over mix**.

On medium heat, preheat a non-stick skillet or griddle, having greased the surface lightly with oil. Pour the desired amount of batter into the pan, and turn when surface bubbles and edges become slightly firm. Repeat until all the batter is used up, keeping the pancakes warm until ready to serve with the pineapple sauce.

Potato and sweet potato cakes with crispy bacon

Serves 6

I serve this dish with the cakes stacked tall, and a dollop of sour cream and chopped chives for added flavor.

INGREDIENTS

1½ lb potatoes

8 oz sweet potatoes

1 small onion, chopped and blanched

1 tbsp olive oil

1 tbsp butter

12 slices cooked crispy bacon, cut into bite-size pieces

PREPARATION

Boil the potatoes and sweet potatoes for 10 minutes and allow to cool in their skins. Peel and grate coarsely. Add the blanched onion and season with sea salt and pepper.

In a heavy non-stick skillet, heat the oil and butter. When hot add the desired quantity of potato mixture. Cook over a low heat until golden and crispy (about 10 minutes). Flip and cook for another 10 minutes. Drain on paper towels. Repeat until all the potato mixture is used up, keeping the cooked potato cakes warm. Serve with the crispy bacon.

Sorrel drink

INGREDIENTS

3 cups dried sorrel, washed thoroughly

1 piece of fresh ginger

peel of ½ orange

6 whole cloves

1¼ cups white sugar

1 small cinnamon stick

5 cups boiling water

PREPARATION

Put all the ingredients except the water into a stainless-steel bowl. Pour the boiling water over and stir. Allow to sit out at room temperature for 12 hours, then refrigerate for 24 hours. Strain through a cheese cloth and serve over ice.

Serves 6

Refreshingly different, with a slightly tart taste, this drink is often served during the Christmas season, with a natural goodness for one's body and soul.

School Days are Happy Days

CHAPTER TWO

School Days are Happy Days:
Two, Four, Six, Eight . . . Let's Eat

The uniformed schoolchildren running across the cricket fields break the silence of every Mustique morning . . . and for those of us lucky enough to share time on the island with them, the schoolyard sounds bring us back – just a little – to our own carefree youth.

The quaint little school on Mustique teaches a few dozen children of all ages and grades every day. For me, this chapter is a fun interlude, as feeding children so often includes lots of the goodies and snacks I would have made for my own children had they grown up here.

For this chapter, I ran a competition requesting island sketches from the older children, judged by resident Mustique artist Patsy Fisher. As well as the winning sketch by student Julianna Ashton, we have included a few other artistic submissions . . . along with our favorite and delicious Mustique recipes for kids!

Recipes

Pineapple and papaya squares | Ginger snap cookies | Banana bread with coconut

Chocolate chunk cookies | Lemon poppy seed cake | Coconut, guava, and almond bars

Peanut butter and guava jelly sandwiches | Ginger beer | Tropical lime cooler

Ginger tea | Tropical fruit punch

Pineapple and papaya squares

INGREDIENTS

Crust:
1¼ cups unsalted butter, softened
½ cup white sugar
½ tsp vanilla extract
¼ tsp sea salt
2²/₃ cups all-purpose flour

Filling:
2 cups chopped pineapple
2 cups chopped and seeded papaya
¾ cup chopped mango
1 cup dark brown sugar
½ cup orange juice
1 cinnamon stick
½ tsp each of grated orange and lemon zest
¹/₈ tsp ground cloves

PREPARATION

Preheat oven to 350°F.

To prepare the crust, beat the butter, sugar, vanilla, and sea salt on low speed with an electric mixer until combined. Add the flour, beating just until the dough comes together. Form two dough balls, one slightly larger than the other; flatten out into two squares, cover and chill for 30 minutes.

For the filling, combine all ingredients together in a heavy-bottomed saucepan. Cook over low heat until reduced to about 2 cups, which will take approximately 1–2 hours. Remove the cinnamon stick and allow to cool.

Place the dough squares on a greased baking sheet and bake for 15–20 minutes until light golden brown. Pour the cooled filling onto the bottom crust, and top with second crust. If preferred, the top crust can be cut into a lattice pattern so the filling shows through. Cut into 12 equal-sized squares.

Makes 12 large squares

These are dangerously addictive, so be aware!

Ginger snap cookies

INGREDIENTS

1 cup white sugar

¾ cup shortening

½ cup molasses

1 egg

2 tsp baking soda

2 cups unbleached white flour

1 tsp ground cloves

1 tbsp powdered ginger

½ tsp sea salt

PREPARATION

Preheat oven to 375°F.

Mix together thoroughly the sugar, shortening, molasses, egg, and baking soda. Then add the flour, spices, and salt and mix until combined. Using a small ice cream scoop, portion out evenly-sized pieces, form each into a ball, and roll in some white sugar. Place on a lightly greased cookie sheet, and bake for 10–12 minutes. Transfer to a cooling rack.

Serves 8

This quantity will serve eight hungry kids...although loved by adults and children alike!

Oliver Milsom

Banana bread with coconut

INGREDIENTS

8 very ripe bananas

4 cups all-purpose flour

$\frac{1}{8}$ tsp sea salt

1½ tsp baking soda

1 tsp grated nutmeg

1 cup unsalted butter, softened

2 cups white sugar

1 egg

3 tbsp dark rum

2 tbsp molasses

1 cup dried, shredded unsweetened coconut

3 tbsp brown sugar

PREPARATION

Preheat oven to 350°F. Butter two 9 x 5 inch loaf pans.

Puree the bananas in a blender. In a medium bowl, combine the flour, salt, baking soda, and nutmeg; set aside.

In an electric mixer, beat the butter and white sugar until light and fluffy, then add the egg, rum, and molasses to blend. Add the banana mixture, and then add the flour mixture, 1 cup at a time, and blend until smooth. Stir in the coconut.

Spoon the batter evenly between the two buttered pans, sprinkle each with the brown sugar, and bake for 1 hour, or until golden brown. Let cool for 20 minutes, and turn onto a wire rack to cool completely.

Serves 12

Jeffrey Alford and Naomi Duguid's book *Home Baking* inspired this marvelous bread. I've adjusted this only slightly for personal preference.

Cerelia Trimmingham

Chocolate chunk cookies

Makes 30 large cookies

Always a hit at any gathering, and always the first to disappear!

INGREDIENTS

1 cup unsalted butter

1 cup brown sugar

2 eggs

1 tsp vanilla extract

2½ cups unbleached white flour

2 cups oatmeal, blended to a fine powder

pinch of sea salt

1 tsp baking powder

2 tsp baking soda

1½ lb semi-sweet chocolate chunks

1 cup chopped walnuts

PREPARATION

Preheat oven to 375°F.

In an electric mixer, beat the butter and sugar until creamy. On low speed, add the eggs and vanilla, then add the flour, oatmeal, sea salt, baking powder, and baking soda. Add the chocolate chunks and nuts.

Using a large ice-cream scoop, place portions of the mixture on a lightly greased cookie sheet a few inches apart (you will probably need more than one cookie sheet, or you can bake the cookies in batches). Bake for 10–12 minutes then transfer to a cooling rack.

Eat and enjoy!

Lemon poppy seed cake

Makes one 9 x 5 inch loaf cake

Taking advantage of our citrus harvest!

INGREDIENTS

3 tbsp poppy seeds

½ cup milk

5 tbsp unsalted butter, softened

1 cup white sugar

2 large eggs

1½ cups unbleached all-purpose flour

1¼ tsp baking powder

grated zest of 2 lemons

¼ tsp sea salt

Lemon syrup:

¼ cup sugar

¼ cup fresh lemon juice

PREPARATION

Preheat oven to 325°F. Grease a 9 x 5 inch loaf pan.

In a small bowl, combine the poppy seeds and milk, and let stand for 1 hour.

In an electric mixer, beat together the butter and sugar until creamy. Add the eggs one at a time and set aside. In a separate bowl, combine the flour, baking powder, lemon zest, and sea salt.

Julianna Ashton

Alternate mixing the poppy seed mixture and the flour mixture into the butter. Beat until smooth. Spoon the mixture into the prepared loaf pan. Bake for about 1 hour, or until a toothpick inserted into the middle of the loaf comes out clean. Transfer to a cooling rack.

Coconut, guava, and almond bars

INGREDIENTS

Crust:
1½ cups unsalted butter, softened
½ cup white sugar
½ tsp vanilla extract
¼ tsp sea salt
2⅔ cups all-purpose flour

Filling:
1½ cups guava jelly
1 cup packaged sweetened coconut
½ tsp grated nutmeg
¼ tsp allspice
¼ cup chopped blanched almonds
1 tsp ground cinnamon
¼ tsp vanilla extract
2 tsp water

Topping:
4 egg whites, at room temperature
⅓ cup granulated sugar

PREPARATION

Preheat oven to 375°F.

For the crust, on low speed, beat together the butter, sugar, vanilla, and sea salt just until blended. Gradually add the flour, beating just until the dough comes together. Cover and chill for 30 minutes. Roll out the dough and place in an 11 x 7 inch baking pan, allowing the crust to go up the sides a little. Place in the preheated oven and cook for 25 minutes, or until golden brown. Allow to cool.

For the filling, mix together all the ingredients and spread evenly over the cooled crust.

For the topping, preheat oven to 350°F. Whip together the egg whites and sugar until soft peaks form. Spread the meringue over the filling, and bake for 20–25 minutes, or until a rich golden brown.

Allow to cool, then cut into squares.

Makes 12 large squares

A wonderful trio of
Caribbean flavors…

Madeline Bunbury Lagoon

Peanut butter and guava jelly sandwiches

Serves 4

Gooey, messy and always fun and tasty.

INGREDIENTS

2 tbsp unsalted butter, softened

8 thick-cut slices of white bread

peanut butter

guava jelly

PREPARATION

Butter the slices of bread. Spread half the slices with peanut butter. Top with a generous dollop of guava jelly and spread. Cover the peanut butter and jelly with the remaining slices of white bread.

Cut each sandwich in half and place in a brown paper bag with lots of napkins for a favorite lunchtime treat.

Ginger beer

INGREDIENTS
8 cups water
1 lb fresh peeled ginger
zest of 1 lime
zest of 1 orange
1¼ lb white sugar
1 cinnamon stick
6 whole cloves
1 star anise

PREPARATION
Bring the water to a boil. Crush the ginger with a kitchen mallet, add to the boiling water, and simmer over medium heat for 20 minutes. Add the remaining ingredients, stir, cover, and remove from heat. Set aside at room temperature for 24 hours, then strain and refrigerate.

Serve chilled, adding soda water if you wish, for a refreshing carbonated taste.

Serves 8

Imagine this on a hot summer day to transport yourself back to a warm Caribbean sun. Refreshingly flavorful and good!

Tropical lime cooler

INGREDIENTS
2 cups fresh lime juice
4 cups sparkling water
sugar or honey

PREPARATION
Combine the lime juice and sparkling water, then sweeten with sugar or honey to taste. If desired, serve over ice with a slice of lime. Refreshing!

Serves 6

The lime trees in my garden serve me well… and there is always an abundance for endless flavorful desserts and concoctions. Kids especially love this drink after school or the playground.

Early Days

When my husband and I swam ashore from our honeymoon boat in 1968, we didn't realize the effect Mustique would have on our lives. Back then it was primitive, but such fun. The electrics went off every evening – a yell for Junior – and somehow we continued to party. There was no set formula to the days: whoever gave the party, everyone on the island just knew about it! It was basic, but completely unstuffy. We had a great "dressing-up" box for charades, which were taken seriously – well, as serious as a group could be, trying to outdo another team while giggling and taking the "piss."

Colin Tennant was very much at the fore of the "theatre." On one occasion, Bianca Jagger had just landed on the island for the first time, and a party ensued at Macaroni Beach. Colin was very much the "master of ceremonies," when Bianca arrived in the clearing under a mosquito net, the ends of which were attached to six naked local men's ankles! Colin leapt forward and, with a slash of a machete, ripped the netting, after which she stepped into the "arena," and did the "dance of the seven veils." After the jollification, there was a lull. Colin shouted, "Right everybody – it's a Paul-Jones," with the men on the inside, and the women on the outside. When the music stopped the first time, Lady Honor was opposite the most well-endowed naked man! As befits a Guinness, she just danced with him! Many such incidents, many such parties.

When our dear friend Virginia Royston sadly died, I organized a playground to be constructed in her memory. When all the stuff arrived from the U.K. and we needed people to erect it and make the whole thing a reality, I put notices up in the office and the village asking for help at 7 a.m. I really wasn't certain if anyone would turn up, but well they did – and by 3 o'clock the playground was finished, and everyone that helped did so because Virginia had helped them. I rang Sun Mitchell, the Prime Minister, and he flew over and officially opened it all in the same day!

The strength of community was extraordinary. Our children were brought up roaming Mustique, and we never worried about where they were, as all the locals knew them, and, if necessary, brought them home. Times have changed – people have died or moved away – but it is still such a magical place.

Diana Heimann

Ginger tea

INGREDIENTS

1 large piece of fresh ginger

4 cups water

sugar or honey

PREPARATION

Peel the ginger, and then crush with a kitchen mallet. In a medium saucepan, bring the water to a boil, add the ginger, and simmer for 10 minutes. Remove the ginger and strain. Add sugar or honey to suit your palate. Serve hot or cool, poured over ice in tall chilled glasses.

Serves 4

Ginger is readily available in all the Grenadine Islands, and its unique and spicy flavor makes this simple drink satisfying for all ages. Serve it either hot or chilled over ice.

Tropical fruit punch

INGREDIENTS

1 cup mango nectar

1 cup papaya nectar

1 cup pineapple juice

1 cup orange juice

1 bottle sparkling water or soda water

juice from 3 passion fruits

grenadine syrup for color (optional)

sugar, to taste

PREPARATION

Mix all the ingredients well, and serve cold over ice.

Serves 6

Sssssh . . . and it's healthy, too! A favorite libation for my kids . . . taking advantage of the fresh tropical fruit juices available almost everywhere.

A Beach "Lime"

CHAPTER THREE

A Beach "Lime": A Beach Barbecue among Friends

When I lived on the island of Mustique year-round, Sunday was always a sacred day – a day of rest and play. While many headed for church for their morning worship, I was usually concocting my first drink, a spicy Bloody Mary or a rum and coke, while contemplating the day ahead… sometimes planned, but often totally spontaneous – always with friends, acquaintances, or my kids. Mostly we would meet at one of Mustique's

wonderful beaches, where we would commence our "liming," enjoying the natural vibe and beauty of the day. Great cocktails, juices, cold beer, potluck dishes, a kick-ass barbecue, accompanied by great music on a bad boom box … along with local gossip and energetic games of ultimate Frisbee, stunt kites, volleyball, or boules.

Here is a sampling of some of the favorite and different dishes we would bring to our own beach "lime." Enjoy!

Recipes

Baked Caribbean christophene | Breadfruit salad | Carambola barbecued chicken legs |

Chicken mumbo jumbo | Pigeon peas with rice | Roasted breadfruit

Snooky's hardcore rum punch | Garden greens and hibiscus flower salad with passion fruit vinaigrette

Jerk baby back ribs | Slow-roasted jerked lamb leg | Caribbean coo-coo

Grilled spicy beef tenderloin | Quinoa and mango salad

Baked Caribbean christophene

INGREDIENTS

3 christophenes, halved, skin on

1 tbsp olive oil

1 onion, finely chopped

2 garlic cloves, chopped

2 tomatoes, diced

1 tsp chopped fresh oregano

6 oz Monterey Jack cheese with jalapeño or medium cheddar, grated

2 tsp coarse cornmeal

PREPARATION

Preheat oven to 350°F.

Cook the christophenes in boiling sea-salted water until tender (about 20 minutes). Cool, remove the seeds, and scoop out the flesh and chop coarsely, leaving the skins intact.

Heat the olive oil in a skillet. Add the onion and garlic and cook until translucent. Add the tomatoes and oregano, and continue cooking until most of the liquid in the pan has evaporated, then stir in the christophene flesh. Add sea salt and pepper to taste.

On a cookie sheet, put the christophene mixture back into the shells, and sprinkle with grated cheese and cornmeal.

Bake for 20–25 minutes, or until lightly browned.

Serves 6

Such a simple vegetable, christophene is native to Latin America, and is a member of the squash family. Historically, this squash was one of the primary foods of the Aztecs and Mayas, and is known in the States and Europe as chayote or mirliton. This dish is perfect to bring to a beach barbecue, as it retains its heat well, has a wonderful aroma, and is of course…delicious!

Breadfruit salad

Serves a very hungry group of friends

This is a really good change from a potato salad. Breadfruit is a wonderful food source, harvested twice a year from trees that grow up to 85 feet! Widely available in the Caribbean, it can also be found in specialty food stores elsewhere in the world, and has a soft, sweetly fragrant flesh that somewhat resembles a sweet squash. It can be cooked in a variety of ways, from roasting to boiled, mashed, and baked, or even as crispy fried chips.

INGREDIENTS

1 whole breadfruit
½ cup diced celery
¼ cup finely diced red onion
1 cup thinly sliced green onion
1 cup diced green sweet pepper
2 cups mayonnaise
2 tbsp Dijon mustard
3 tbsp hot sauce
4 tbsp chopped cilantro
½ tbsp white wine vinegar
½ tbsp sugar
1 cup chopped crispy cooked bacon
cilantro sprigs, to garnish

PREPARATION

Cut the breadfruit into quarters, and cook in boiling sea-salted water until softened, but still firm, approximately 15 minutes. Remove from the water and allow to cool. Peel, core, and cut into cubes.

In a large stainless-steel bowl, mix the breadfruit cubes and all the remaining ingredients (except the bacon). Season with sea salt and pepper to taste, sprinkle with the bacon pieces, and garnish with a few cilantro sprigs. Serve at room temperature.

Carambola barbecued chicken legs

INGREDIENTS
4 tbsp of your favorite Caribbean seasoning mix
3 tbsp vegetable oil
12 chicken legs, halved
carambola and lime slices, to garnish

Glaze:
3 carambolas, blended
¼ cup lime juice
½ cup honey
2 tbsp chopped parsley
2 tbsp chopped cilantro
2 tbsp white wine vinegar
1 tbsp soy sauce
1 tbsp chopped garlic
1 tbsp hot sauce (optional)

PREPARATION
Combine the seasoning and oil, and baste the chicken well. Set aside for 20 minutes at room temperature to let the flavors set.

Whisk all the ingredients for the glaze together until well combined, and set aside.

Prepare the barbecue. Grill the chicken over medium coals for about 25 minutes, turning occasionally and brushing with the carambola glaze after each turn.

Transfer to a platter and garnish with fresh carambola and lime slices.

Serves 8

Carambola is known by many different names. In St. Vincent and the Grenadines, we call it starfruit or "five fingers," due to its five-sided star shape. It has yellow glossy skin and juicy citrus flesh, and is a great flavor to add to chicken.

Chicken mumbo jumbo

INGREDIENTS

4 tbsps olive oil

1 red sweet pepper, deseeded and sliced

1 green sweet pepper, deseeded and sliced

1 yellow or orange sweet pepper, deseeded and sliced

3 onions, sliced

6 boneless chicken breasts, cut into strips

2 tbsp seasoning mix

2 generous splashes Wreck-tum Fire or other brand chili oil

4 tbsp dark rum

1 tbsp chopped fresh ginger

2 garlic cloves, chopped

1 tsp grated lemon zest

2 tsp Wreck-tum Fire Green or any mild hot sauce

juice of 1 lemon

sea salt and pepper

ginger soy sauce (optional)

PREPARATION

Over the barbecue, pour the olive oil into a large cast-iron skillet. When hot, fry all the sliced peppers together with the onions. Remove while the peppers are still crunchy, together with the oil.

Season the chicken strips with seasoning mix. Reheat the pan until very hot; add the chili oil and chicken. When half cooked, flame with dark rum.

Add all the other ingredients, including the oil with the peppers and onions. Stir well and continue cooking until the chicken is just cooked and very moist, 1–2 minutes. Check seasoning and drizzle with ginger soy before serving, if desired.

Serves 8

A beautiful dish of seared chicken with a "traffic light" of fresh peppers, created by Kevin Snook and Captain Phil. This is a great dish to "show off" with last-minute cooking, lots of color, and even flames.

Pigeon peas with rice

Serves 6

A traditional Creole dish, this is an excellent accompaniment to any main course of meat or fish. Pigeon peas are native to India, and their sweet taste is similar to sugar snap peas.

INGREDIENTS

2 tbsp olive oil

1 onion, chopped

1 garlic clove, chopped

1 cup chopped green sweet pepper

1 small carrot, peeled and diced

1 tomato, diced

½ tsp chopped scotch bonnet pepper

2 cups long grain rice, washed and drained

2 tins pigeon peas, drained

4 cups coconut milk (see Note)

1 bay leaf

sea salt

PREPARATION

Preheat oven to 350°F.

In a thick-bottomed wide pan, heat the oil and cook the onion, garlic, and green pepper for 5–7 minutes, or until the onion is translucent.

Add all the other ingredients, mix well, and place the pan, covered, in the oven for about 40 minutes.

NOTE

For coconut milk: using a mature coconut, crack open the dark fibrous shell and release the coconut water. Using a sharp knife, separate the luscious white flesh from the shell and grate it. To make a rich coconut milk, blend the grated flesh and 1½ cups hot water (less for a thicker milk). Strain through a fine sieve or cheese cloth, pushing through to obtain as much milk as possible. (This can be frozen for future use.)

Both coconut milk and coconut water are low in fat and calories and contain no cholesterol.

Roasted breadfruit

INGREDIENTS

2 breadfruits

butter, to serve

PREPARATION

Prepare a fire with local wood; allow to burn until embers are hot and most of the flame has gone. Place the breadfruits in their skin on the coals, turning every so often until all the skin has become black and the breadfruits are soft and cooked.

Remove from the coals and scrape off the black residue. Peel and cut each breadfruit into quarters using a sharp knife, remove the core, and serve with some butter, sprinkling with sea salt and freshly ground pepper.

Serves 8

This humble vegetable was brought to the West Indies from the Pacific isles by Captain Bligh in 1789. The many plants aboard HMS *Bounty* were swiftly distributed around these islands. Definitely a staple of everyone's food and diet, this popular dish is always a great conversation piece at any beach barbecue.

Serves 8

If making a classic rum punch, my rule is ratios of 1 part sour, 1 part sweet, 3 parts strong, and 4 parts weak. I often replace the water with unsweetened tropical juices. This version is just a bit stronger.

Snooky's hardcore rum punch

INGREDIENTS

1 cup lime juice – *sour*

1 cup sugar syrup – *sweet*

2½ cups dark rum – *strong*

½ cup strong white rum – *strong*

2½ cups water – *weak*

dash of Angostura bitters

freshly grated nutmeg

PREPARATION

Mix all the ingredients together, with the exception of the nutmeg. Fill each glass with ice, pour over the punch, and sprinkle with nutmeg.

Garden greens and hibiscus flower salad with passion fruit vinaigrette

INGREDIENTS

1 large head of lettuce or a mix of different lettuces, washed and loosely torn into smaller pieces

1 large handful of baby spinach leaves, washed and torn

1 small cucumber, peeled, deseeded and thinly sliced

6 red hibiscus flowers, picked into individual petals

Vinaigrette:

3 tbsp extra virgin olive oil

3 tbsp vegetable oil

1 tbsp cider vinegar

3 tbsp fresh passion fruit juice

1 tsp Dijon mustard

1 small garlic clove, chopped

sea salt and pepper

PREPARATION

In a stainless-steel bowl, mix all the salad ingredients together. Meanwhile, whisk the vinaigrette ingredients. Pour over salad and toss just before serving. You may have more vinaigrette than you desire – just store in the refrigerator.

Serves 6

The delicate flavor these gorgeous flowers impart is naturally enhanced with the sweetness of honey. Simply sublime!

Jerk baby back ribs

INGREDIENTS

8 portions baby back pork ribs

Jerk:

12 whole black peppercorns, ground

6 whole allspice seeds, ground

1 small onion, finely chopped

2 tbsp chopped thyme leaves

⅛ tsp ground cloves

½ tsp chopped scotch bonnet pepper

2 tbsp lime juice

2 tbsp dark rum

sea salt, to taste

2 tbsp olive oil

PREPARATION

Blend all the jerk ingredients together and rub well into the pork. Allow to marinate, refrigerated, for 2 hours.

Prepare the barbecue for grilling. Wipe excess marinade from the ribs, and cook on a hot grill for approximately 5–7 minutes per side.

For extra flavor, add hardwood chips to the barbecue, such as apple, hickory, or mesquite.

Serves 8

Flavorful and juicy jerk meat, marinated with onions, allspice, chilies, and rum, originates from Jamaica. It is typically cooked over a smoky fire using exotic woods, variations of which can be found all over the Caribbean.

Slow-roasted jerked lamb leg

Serves 8

To appreciate the true jerk flavor, allow the lamb to marinate overnight before cooking. The lamb goes great with guava jelly.

INGREDIENTS

1 leg of lamb, on the bone

4 tbsp jerk seasoning rub

1 tsp coarse sea salt

PREPARATION

Make incisions into the lamb leg, just piercing the surface. Rub the jerk seasoning and sea salt thoroughly into the lamb. Cover and let marinate overnight.

Before cooking, bring the lamb to room temperature and preheat the oven to 300°F. In a roasting pan, completely surround the lamb with tin foil, and slowly roast for 3 hours. Increase the temperature to 450°F, remove the foil, and continue roasting until the lamb is brown and crisp. Remove from the oven and allow to cool for 20 minutes before carving.

Caribbean coo-coo

INGREDIENTS

6 cups water or mild chicken stock

1 thyme stalk

16 young okra, stemmed and sliced

4 tbsp unsalted butter

1 cup cornmeal

1 cup cooked corn

thyme sprigs, to garnish

PREPARATION

Bring the water or stock to a boil with the thyme. Once boiling, remove the thyme and add the okra, butter, and sea salt to taste. Slowly stir in the cornmeal, and continue stirring over a low flame for 10 minutes. Stir in the corn, and serve in warmed bowls garnished with a sprig of thyme.

Serves 8

Okra serves as the key ingredient for this dish. A member of the hibiscus family, and considered an aphrodisiac, it is a traditional Mustique favorite.

Grilled spicy beef tenderloin

INGREDIENTS

8 garlic cloves, minced

2 tbsp hot mustard

2 tbsp of your favorite all-purpose seasoning spice

2 lb beef tenderloin, trimmed

oil

PREPARATION

Rub the garlic, mustard, and seasoning into the tenderloin. Allow to marinate for 2–3 hours.

Preheat your broiler to high or prepare the barbecue. Remove the excess marinade from the tenderloin and season with sea salt and freshly ground black pepper. Brush with a little oil and begin to cook, turning on all sides, allowing 10–12 minutes for medium rare. Enjoy!

Serves 8

Great for the beach, this can be prepared ahead and served cold or grilled last minute. Nice with a crisp summer salad.

Ten Days in Mustique

We were awoken just after dawn by the sound of an outboard motor coming into L'Ansecoy Bay. This was most unusual, even more so when we saw a fisherman's boat landing four men on the beach near our house and then tying up to our mooring buoy. Who were these men, walking on the sand, carrying shoes in their hands? No fishermen wore shoes.

"Is this Union Island?" one asked. "Where are we? Can we buy petrol? Can we change our clothes?"

The four men, in their twenties or thirties, along with their boatman, used our garden shelter to change. We gave them some water. To get them petrol, we phoned the Security man, who came over in his truck to take them to the village until the petrol station opened at 7 a.m. He parked on the village hill at a place that happened to be outside the Police House. All five men jumped from the truck and ran off.

A little while later the boatman returned, and told the police that the other four had grabbed him in St. Vincent and forced him to take them off the island. All four were convicts who had escaped from prison in St. Lucia. Their leader had been convicted of bank robbery and was armed. Was he the one whom I had asked if he had enough cash to buy petrol? Whoever it was, he did.

The next ten days were perhaps the most exciting that Mustique has ever known. St. Vincent sent over the Coast Guard and a troop of men in camouflage uniforms armed with rifles. The convicts were elusive, well able to hide in the brush and emerge only at night, walking into the kitchens of houses to get food.

They were caught one by one, but not without a shooting that seriously injured the second man to be captured. The third man had been hiding under an upturned boat near the construction workers' camp at Granby. They advised him that it would be better to surrender than be shot, which he did.

The fourth, and last, of the convicts was the man who had engineered their escape from the prison in St. Lucia. He had been released from prison but had come back to get his friends. Very resourceful, he was well able to spot traps set for him, such as cotton thread spread amongst the bushes. The militiamen hoped to find the thread that had been broken and, of course, once he saw it, he only had to duck underneath and hide where they would not look. Some house staff wished him well and left out food and water. The search for him went on for days.

People on Mustique did not seem concerned. No one had been threatened or harmed. In fact, the militiamen lurking around with rifles seemed more of a menace. And there seems little doubt that when the last man still at large was eventually seen, no time was wasted in shooting him dead.

For weeks later, as legends grew, we were known as the couple who gave the convicts breakfast.

Rodney and Ouida Touche

Quinoa and mango salad

INGREDIENTS

Dressing:
½ cup extra virgin olive or grapeseed oil
1 garlic clove, chopped
4 tbsp apple cider vinegar
 squeeze of lemon juice
1 tbsp chopped fresh ginger
sea salt and pepper
1 chili pepper, finely chopped
½ cup chopped fresh garden mint

Salad:
2 cups cooked quinoa
2 ripe mangoes, chopped
½ cup chopped celery
1 peeled carrot, grated
1 green onion, thinly sliced
1 red sweet pepper, deseeded and sliced
½ cup sliced toasted almonds

PREPARATION

In a medium bowl, whisk together all the dressing ingredients. In a separate bowl, combine all the salad ingredients. Add the dressing to the salad, mix, and serve.

Serves 6

Nutritious and delicious, this recipe was given to me by my two oldest sons, Chris and Dan. They both love to cook! Quinoa is an ancient grain of the Incas, used as their main protein source. The addition of the fruits and nuts in this recipe offers an excellent source of vitamins A, C, and B6.

The Fisherman's Village

CHAPTER FOUR

The Fisherman's Village: Mustique's Freshest Catch

The Fisherman's Village in Mustique is an integral part of our lives here, a humble and beautiful community that keeps us fed every day with the generous gifts brought in by the fishermen's nets.

Nestled in Britannia Bay, the sandy beach at the Fisherman's Village is a blanket of multicolored fishing boats with a myriad of different names, most of which are built in nearby Bequia.

When our fishermen are not out searching for the freshest harvests, they can be seen repairing their nets, rocking in the hammocks, or playing a passionate game of dominoes with a cold Guinness nearby.

There are still plenty of fish in these waters, including barracuda, red snapper, marlin, and mahi-mahi, to name but a few.

Recipes

Coconut fried shrimp with pineapple salsa | Bul jol | Lorie's full moon Mustique crabs

Seared grouper Creole | Whole baked red snapper with fennel | Fish "tea" with coconut dumplings

Blackened shrimp with mango ginger salsa | Captain Phil's kick-ass seared tuna

Broiled swordfish with avocado chili salsa | Spicy crab cakes with mango chutney

Conch fritters with mustard sauce | River lobster and saffron risotto

Pan-seared tuna with a lime pepper crust and green bean salad

Coconut fried shrimp with pineapple salsa

INGREDIENTS

2 cups all-purpose flour
1½ cups milk
1½ tsp baking powder
½ tsp sea salt
1 tsp seasoning mix
peanut oil for deep-frying
2 lb jumbo shrimp, cleaned and deveined
2 cups grated fresh coconut

Salsa:
1 small fresh ripe pineapple, peeled, cored and diced
1 crunchy green apple, peeled, cored and diced
1 small red onion, thinly sliced
¼ cup chopped cilantro
3 tsp lime juice
2 tsp hot sauce
sea salt and pepper

PREPARATION

Combine all the salsa ingredients and allow to chill.

To make batter, combine 1½ cups flour, the milk, baking powder, sea salt, and seasoning mix in a large bowl.

Meanwhile, heat the peanut oil to 350°F. Dredge each shrimp through the balance of the flour, then dip into the batter and roll in the grated coconut. Fry the shrimp in small batches until brown. Remove and lay on paper towel to absorb excess oil.

Place the shrimp on a serving dish with the pineapple salsa.

Serves 6

The crispy exterior from the coconut and the moist shrimp interior, combined with the sweetness of the pineapple salsa, make this a true winner.

Bul jol

Serves 6

My version of
this traditional
Caribbean salad,
salt fish being its
key ingredient. This
recipe has a very
special place in
the hearts of all the
island people, and
can be a staple in
any home.

INGREDIENTS
8 oz boneless salt fish
1 large tomato, finely diced
1 red onion, deseeded and finely diced
1 green sweet pepper, deseeded and finely diced
½ tsp chopped hot pepper
1 ripe avocado, peeled, pitted and chopped
juice of 2 limes
2 tbsp extra virgin olive oil
dill or parsley, to garnish

PREPARATION
Flake the fish into pieces and soak overnight.
Discard the water and drain the fish well. Mix the fish with the tomato, onion, green pepper, and hot pepper. Add the avocado, lime juice, and olive oil. Add freshly ground pepper to taste and garnish with fresh dill or parsley.

Lorie's full moon Mustique crabs

MUST-HAVES

* Invite some fun friends at full moon
* Serve plenty of rum punches
* Arm guests with flashlights, bug spray, protective gloves, and flour sacks
* Serve more rum punches
* After the guests are well done, proceed to the "crab area"
* Add lots of laughs, and you now have official Mustique "Land Crabs"

PREPARATION

Serve rum punches (not to the crabs). Add bits of lettuce or papaya to a large bin filled with water and add the crabs (add some rum punch for extra flavor, if you wish). Wait 4–6 hours.

Invite some more friends and serve more rum punch. Clean the crabs carefully, taking care with the claws.

Boil a large pot of water, and drop in the crabs. Add a generous portion of callaloo, toss in local seasonings, and boil until done (about 10–12 minutes).

Take to the beach with lots of friends and rum punches. Serve "finger style."

Then finish it all off with a swim in the sea under the "full moon"!

If you want to have a good picnic with old friends, new friends, and friends of friends, think about this recipe!

Seared grouper Creole

Serves 6

A traditional Caribbean favorite.

INGREDIENTS

6 skinless grouper fillets, about 8 oz each

3 tbsp lime juice

2 tbsp olive oil

½ cup flour

2 tbsp melted butter

2 garlic cloves, chopped

2 onions, thinly sliced

2 green sweet peppers, cored, deseeded and thinly sliced

1 yellow sweet pepper, cored, deseeded and thinly sliced

⅓ cup dry white wine

1 bay leaf

2 cups tomato sauce

1½ tsp hot sauce

1 tsp lemon juice

PREPARATION

Rinse the grouper fillets and pat dry. Marinate for 15 minutes in the lime juice, olive oil, and a little sea salt and freshly ground pepper. Dredge with the flour, shaking off any excess.

Add a little oil to a cast-iron pan. When hot, briefly sear both sides of the fish. Transfer to paper towels and drain.

To make the sauce, add the butter, garlic, and onion to the same pan and cook until soft. Add the peppers, white wine, bay leaf, tomato sauce, hot sauce, and the lemon juice. Simmer for about 10 minutes. Season with sea salt and freshly ground pepper to taste.

Add the fish to the sauce and gently simmer for 5 minutes.

Serve with a rice dish.

Whole baked red snapper with fennel

INGREDIENTS

½ cup fresh orange juice

½ cup fresh lime juice

1 tsp grated orange zest

1 tsp grated lime zest

3 tbsp chopped shallots

2 tbsp olive oil

1 whole red snapper, 2–3 lb, cleaned and scaled

1 head of fennel, sliced and blanched

PREPARATION

In a bowl, combine the orange and lime juices, the zest, shallots, and olive oil. Make diagonal incisions in the skin of the red snapper, then add the fish to the marinade. Cover and refrigerate for 45 minutes, turning once or twice.

Preheat the oven to 425°F.

Remove the snapper from the marinade, and place in a baking dish. Add the sliced fennel to the cavity, drizzle a small amount of the marinade over, and cook for about 30 minutes. Transfer from the baking dish to a platter and serve.

Serves 6

An impressive dish to present – and so succulent and tasty as well.

Fish "tea" with coconut dumplings

INGREDIENTS

4 tbsp butter

1 onion, finely chopped

6 garlic cloves

4 green onions, chopped

2 leaves of ticky thyme or ordinary thyme

2 bay leaves

8 cups fish stock

1 large potato, diced

2 cups diced squash

1 cup diced tannia

1 lb okra, halved

1 christophene, peeled and diced

1 whole scotch bonnet pepper

1 lb red snapper, filleted, skinned and cut into 2 inch pieces

1 lb grouper, filleted, skinned and cut into 2 inch pieces

1 lb shrimp or lobster, cut into 1 inch pieces

¼ cup cilantro

Dumplings:

1 cup all-purpose flour

1 tsp sugar

½ tsp baking powder

1 tsp sea salt

½ tsp ground pepper

¼ cup grated fresh coconut

2 tbsp unsalted butter

coconut water (see Note)

PREPARATION

For the dumplings, sift together the dry ingredients and mix in the coconut. Rub in the butter with your fingertips until the dough is crumbly. Add enough coconut water to form a stiff dough. When ready to cook, form pieces of the dough into 1½ inch oblong dumplings.

In a large, heavy-duty pan, melt the butter. Add the onion, garlic, green onions, thyme, and bay leaves. Allow to cook. Add the fish stock and raise the heat to bring to a gentle simmer. Add the diced potato, squash, tannia, okra, christophene, and the scotch bonnet pepper. Add sea salt and freshly ground pepper to taste.

When the root vegetables are almost cooked, add the dumplings. Cook for 10 minutes then add the fish and cook until firm. Remove the whole pepper, sprinkle with cilantro leaves and serve.

NOTE

Coconut water is best obtained from very fresh, immature coconuts direct from the tree, when the meat of the nut is still like jelly. Once coconuts reach their foreign destinations they are brown balls, past their peak. To extract the juice, cut off the pointed end opposite the stem. Locate one of the three "eyes," pierce, and pour the water into a container. Then crack the coconut open and indulge in the gooey gel of the immature nut.

Serves 8

This is like a Caribbean version of the French bouillabaisse. For this dish, I make the fish stock from the leftover bones of a cleaned grouper – throw it all in!

Blackened shrimp with mango ginger salsa

INGREDIENTS
3 lb large shrimp, peeled and deveined
½ cup clarified butter

Blackening seasoning mix:
1 tsp cayenne pepper
1 tsp ground cumin
½ tsp onion powder
1 tsp red pepper flakes
¼ tsp dried thyme
1 tsp ground black pepper
½ tsp garlic powder
½ tsp sea salt
¼ tsp dried oregano

Mango salsa:
2 mangoes, peeled and diced
1 tsp chopped cilantro
1 tsp finely diced green sweet pepper
2 tsp fresh ginger juice (see Note)
1 small red onion, finely diced
1 tbsp fresh lime juice

PREPARATION
Combine all the ingredients for the mango salsa and set aside.

Mix together all the blackening ingredients. Dredge the shrimp in the clarified butter and then coat with the blackening seasoning mix.

Heat a cast-iron pan until very hot. Lay the shrimp flat, taking care not to overcrowd the pan, or thread the shrimp on skewers and place the skewers on the pan. Sear until slightly charred. Turn over and blacken the other side.

Arrange the blackened shrimp on a plate and serve with the mango salsa.

NOTE
To make ginger juice: peel a good-sized piece of fresh ginger and put into a blender with 1 cup warm water. Blend, then strain through a fine sieve. Less water will of course give you a stronger juice, which can easily be frozen in ice-cube trays.

Serves 6

Elegant and easy to prepare, and a wonderful prelude to a good meal.

Captain Phil's kick-ass seared tuna

INGREDIENTS

1⅓ lb yellowfin tuna

2 tbsp Wreck-tum Fire Ginger Soy Sauce

3 tbsp Wreck-tum Fire Chili Oil

1 shallot, finely chopped

1 large piece of fresh ginger, finely chopped

1 tbsp rum

juice of 1 lemon or lime

2 tbsp sesame seeds

PREPARATION

Cut the tuna into 2 inch medallions. Coat the medallions evenly with the soy sauce, sea salt, and pepper.

Place the chili oil in a large pan or skillet. Heat the pan until the oil starts to burn. Add the chopped shallot and ginger and cook for at least 1 minute until golden brown. Place the tuna medallions in the pan. Shake the pan vigorously, cooking for about 30 seconds. Flip the tuna and cook for an additional minute. Add the rum and lemon or lime juice.

Lay the cooked tuna on a plate and coat with sesame seeds on both sides. Serve, hot or cold, with ginger soy sauce for dipping.

Serves 4

It's all about living the dream – and my good friends Phil and Nicola do just that. They run a successful sailboat business, the Splendid Adventure, with a 40-foot catamaran chartering through the idyllic Grenadine Islands. In addition, they produce a famous range of hot sauces called Captain Phil's Wreck-tum Fire, of which I'm an active member of the team. If you don't happen to have a supply of Captain Phil's, pull out your own favorite chili oil and soy sauce.

Broiled swordfish
with avocado chili salsa

Serves 8

The cumin and lime marinade brings this dish alive.

INGREDIENTS

6 swordfish steaks, cut ½ inch thick

Marinade:

3 garlic cloves, chopped

½ cup fresh lime juice

¼ tsp sea salt

¼ tsp ground cumin

freshly ground black pepper

Salsa:

2 red onions, finely sliced

2 large avocados, peeled and sliced

2 ripe red tomatoes, peeled, halved and deseeded

½ red chili, deseeded and diced

juice and zest of 1 lime

sea salt and black pepper, to taste

½ tsp medium hot sauce

3 tbsp chopped cilantro

PREPARATION

Mix all the marinade ingredients together. Pour over the fish steaks and marinate in the refrigerator for 30 minutes.

Combine the salsa ingredients and set aside.

Preheat the broiler until very hot. Remove the swordfish from the marinade and blot dry. Broil for 1 minute on each side.

Present the fish with a generous portion of avocado salsa.

Spicy crab cakes with mango chutney

Serves 6

INGREDIENTS

⅓ cup oil

Crab cakes:
½ cup mayonnaise
½ cup finely chopped onion
1 tsp Worcestershire sauce
½ tsp cayenne pepper
½ tsp sea salt
½ cup finely chopped red sweet pepper
½ cup finely chopped green sweet pepper
1 garlic clove, chopped
½ cup fine cracker crumbs
2 eggs
2 tbsp chopped parsley
2 tbsp chopped cilantro
1 tsp dry mustard powder
1 tsp celery salt
1 tbsp chopped chives
1 lb crabmeat

Coating:
1 cup flour
6 eggs, beaten
1½ cups cornmeal

PREPARATION

In a large bowl, mix all the crab cake ingredients well, adding the crabmeat last, and carefully folding it in until it is all combined. Chill the mixture for 30 minutes in the refrigerator. Shape into cakes.

Roll each cake through the flour, dip into the egg, and finally roll in the cornmeal. Transfer the cakes to a baking sheet until ready to cook.

In a large skillet, heat the oil over medium heat. Pan-fry the cakes until golden brown – about 3 minutes on each side. When cooked, place on paper towel to drain and serve immediately with a small dollop of mango chutney.

Makes 4 cups

Another Caribbean favorite, enhanced by the wonderful flavor that mangoes impart.

Mango chutney

INGREDIENTS

$1/3$ cup brown sugar

½ cup white wine vinegar

juice of 1 lemon

½ cup chopped red sweet pepper

½ cup chopped green sweet pepper

2 garlic cloves

½ tsp ground cinnamon

½ tsp ground cloves

½ tsp powdered ginger

½ tsp chili powder

¼ lsp ground coriander

¼ cup raisins

4 large mangoes, peeled and cubed

PREPARATION

In a large saucepan, combine all the ingredients except the mangoes and bring the mixture to a boil. Add the mangoes to the pan and cook slowly for about 30 minutes until tender.

Store in the refrigerator for up to a month or pour into sterilized jars until ready to use.

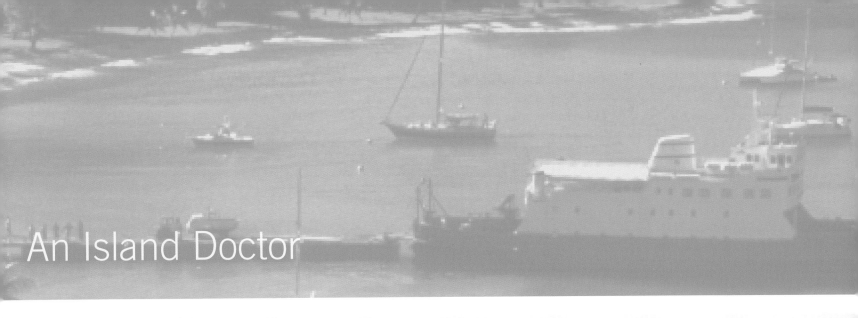

An Island Doctor

 the only doctor on a small and remote island, I have experienced some unique and often very amusing scenarios.

One such was on the evening of New Year's Eve. We were all looking forward to a fun-filled evening, with first a cocktail party and then moving on to the island New Year's party.

Understandably I was somewhat annoyed to get a telephone message from Basil's Bar from someone on a yacht. There was a fellow yachtie who had dislocated his shoulder and could I come and see him? The caller was German and spoke little English and the conversation became more confused. In desperation, I agreed to come to the boat to see the patient. I would have preferred for the patient to come to the clinic but I was told this was impossible.

I set off feeling rather bullied into the situation, as it would have been better medical practice to see the patient in the clinic, especially as I would probably need to give him an anesthetic to reduce the pain. So, having collected a large amount of heavy equipment, I set off for the jetty.

On arrival, I was met by two men who helped me and my two large equipment bags into the smallest excuse for a dinghy that I have ever seen. It consisted of an inflatable ring the size of a bathtub and a mesh for the floor that meant I was paddling in seawater above my ankles.

As we set off, I was becoming increasingly annoyed by the realization that I was missing a champagne-soaked party, only to then have the heavens open, starting to pour rain on our sorry heads. This would not have been a problem, except for the fact that the rubber ring had to be rowed and they had only one paddle. Furthermore, that night there were over 170 yachts in the harbor and the visibility was appalling, so quite naturally we got lost. It was 40 minutes later that we eventually found the boat, which was a small rental catamaran. Clambering out, I was glad to get into the dry and warm. The joy of reaching the boat lasted less than ten seconds, as I looked around the cabin at a group of middle-aged Germans, all of whom were delighted to see me but all of whom were completely naked and made no effort to cover themselves on my arrival. I felt that there must be a hidden camera somewhere but came to the realization that real life can be stranger than even anything *Candid Camera* can dream up.

Feeling a combination of annoyance and embarrassment I was shown to the patient. He was also naked but was stuck in the top bunk of a tiny cabin. I realized that there was no alternative but to get very intimate and clamber into bed with him.

At this point my frustration took over, and without giving any anesthetic I got myself into a position that came from an illustration in the *Kama Sutra* and wrestled his shoulder back into place. A reassuring "clunk" and I knew I was on my way back to champagne and canapés – maybe a little bit late but well deserved.

Michael Bunbury

Conch fritters with mustard sauce

INGREDIENTS

2 cups ground conch meat

1 tbsp lemon juice

¼ cup finely diced celery

¼ cup finely diced carrot

¼ cup finely diced green sweet pepper

2 tsp baking powder

2 tsp chopped parsley

1 garlic clove, finely chopped

½ tsp cayenne pepper

2 eggs

2 tsp Worcestershire sauce

6 tbsp milk

sea salt, to taste

1 cup all-purpose flour

2 cups peanut oil

Mustard sauce

1 cup mayonnaise

2 tbsp Dijon mustard

2 tbsp fresh lime juice

¼ tsp lime zest

1 tbsp Tabasco sauce

1 tbsp Worcestershire sauce

1 tbsp green seasoning (see Note)

sea salt and pepper, to taste

PREPARATION

Adding the flour last, mix all the ingredients except the peanut oil together well and allow the mixture to rest in the refrigerator for a couple of hours before cooking. It is important to use cold batter when cooking.

Heat the peanut oil in a skillet on a medium heat until the oil is about 350°F. Carefully drop spoonfuls of the batter into the oil, according to the desired size of fritter. (I use a tablespoon as a guideline for canapé-sized fritters.) Allow to brown on all sides, turning if necessary. Drain on paper towels and serve with a side dish of mustard sauce.

For the mustard sauce, mix all the ingredients together. This sauce will improve if allowed to sit for a couple of days. Keep in the refrigerator.

NOTE

Caribbean green seasoning is a cornerstone of tasty West Indian cookery and can be found everywhere throughout the Caribbean and in West Indian markets around the world. It is primarily a mix of green onions, garlic, herbs, spices, and hot peppers and it is used to season fish, meat, dips, stocks, sauces...you name it.

Serves 6

Conch is very popular in Mustique and has a mild sweet taste. Often it is regarded as an aphrodisiac – judge for yourself!

River lobster and saffron risotto

Serves 6

This recipe was given to me by my good friend Rahul Chakraborty, a very talented chef who's making a name for himself with his new restaurant, Elephant, in the small village of Grenville, Quebec, Canada.

INGREDIENTS

1 tsp saffron threads

¼ cup hot water

¼ cup olive oil

2 garlic cloves, crushed

3 tablespoons chopped chives

1½ lb river lobster (large prawns), peeled, deveined and diced, plus 4 whole, deveined, to garnish

¼ cup dry sherry

¼ cup white wine

6 cups fish stock

1 onion, finely chopped

2 cups risotto rice

handful of green peas

2 tbsp butter

PREPARATION

Soak the saffron threads in the hot water.

Heat half the oil in a saucepan. Add the garlic, chives, and diced river lobster and season with sea salt and pepper. Cook for 1 minute, and then add the sherry, wine, and saffron with the liquid. Remove the river lobster with a slotted spoon and set aside. Simmer until the liquid has reduced by half. Pour in the fish stock together with 1 cup water, cover and keep at a constant simmer.

In a separate large heavy-based saucepan, heat the remaining oil. Cook the onion for 3 minutes, or until a light golden. Add the rice and stir over medium heat for 3 minutes to toast the rice.

Add ½ cup of the stock in the pan to the rice and stir constantly with a wooden spoon over low heat until all the liquid has been absorbed. Add another ½ cup stock and repeat the process until all the stock has been added and the rice is tender and creamy – this will take 25–30 minutes. Add a little water if needed. Add the diced lobster, the peas, and butter and stir until heated through.

Meanwhile, steam, broil, or grill the four whole river lobsters.

Season the risotto to taste and garnish with the whole river lobsters, then serve.

Pan-seared tuna with a lime pepper crust and green bean salad

Serves 4

My version of
the classic salad
Niçoise.

INGREDIENTS
8 oz lightly blanched green beans

2 tbsp chopped parsley

½ red onion, finely chopped

1½ lb tuna fillets

1 lb purple or white new potatoes, skins on, cooked and sliced

2 tomatoes, peeled, cut into 8 segments

20 black olives, pitted

sun dried tomato and yellow pepper oils (optional)

Marinade:

juice and zest of 1 lime

1 tbsp coarse-ground black pepper

¼ tsp sea salt

1 tbsp olive oil

Vinaigrette:

2 tbsp fresh lemon juice ¼ tsp sea salt

2 tbsp red wine vinegar ¼ tsp freshly ground black pepper

2 tbsp Dijon mustard ¾ cup extra virgin olive oil

2 anchovy fillets, chopped pinch of sugar (optional)

1 tbsp chopped garlic

PREPARATION
For the vinaigrette, in a small bowl, whisk together the lemon juice, vinegar, mustard, anchovies, garlic, sea salt, and pepper. Slowly add the olive oil, continuing to whisk until emulsified and add sugar if desired. Pour into an empty bottle, and refrigerate until ready to use.

Toss together the blanched green beans, parsley, and chopped red onion; add desired amount of vinaigrette.

Rinse the tuna fillet and pat dry with a cloth. In a bowl, combine all the marinade ingredients together. Rub the marinade onto the tuna to coat well.

Using a cast-iron pan, heat on medium high. Add the tuna and sear on all sides – about 1 minute in total, to allow the tuna to stay rare.

To assemble the dish, arrange the potato slices on the bottom of the plates and randomly add the tomato and a generous helping of the bean vinaigrette. Slice the seared tuna while hot, or leave the fillets whole, and lay on top of the beans. Scatter the plate with black olives and drizzle with sun dried tomato and yellow pepper oils if desired. Serve immediately.

Dressing Up Mustique

CHAPTER FIVE

Dressing Up Mustique: Themed Parties

Indulgence on Mustique comes naturally, inspired by its surroundings and its lively group of homeowners and their guests. Mustique gatherings – and the nearly constant themed parties from one end of the island to the other – demand a great deal of creativity and imagination. Here's just a sampling of events I've catered for: a construction party, where guests were given hardhats upon arrival, salads were presented in toy Tonka trucks, and bread passed in tin buckets…a 90th birthday party on Macaroni Beach, with paella prepared

five

on an open barbecue for 100 guests…once, the daughter of the Prime Minister celebrated her ninth birthday with a Ricky Martin theme…and yet another party was billed as a "Seafood Orgy" for a group of very sexy women. In addition, there are sushi parties, Thai evenings, holiday parties, and so on. The list is, of course, as endless as one's imagination.

We broke this chapter down into three different themed party menus: Thai, Paella, and Pizza – they would all work well for many different party scenarios, on Mustique, or off.

Recipes

Thai One On: An Asian Feast

Ginger shrimp and lemongrass broth | Asian marinated vegetables | Seared beef flank steak pad Thai with toasted cashews

Paella Beachside Barbi

Spanish-style paella | Arugula salad with cherry tomatoes and red onion

Focaccia bread with black and green olives | Summertime sangria with a Caribbbean twist

Pizza Party

Roasted artichoke and buffalo mozzarella pizza with chili oil | Smoked salmon, baby spinach, and Brie pizza with caper berries

Caesar salad with ciabatta croutons and shaved Parmesan

Ginger shrimp and lemon grass broth

INGREDIENTS

2 lb medium shrimp, peeled and deveined

1½ tbsp grated lime zest

⅓ cup lime juice

1½ tbsp ground coriander

1½ tbsp chopped fresh ginger

1 tbsp olive oil

½ cup finely chopped onion

½ cup finely chopped celery

3 cups shrimp stock

2 cups coconut milk

1 cup 2% milk

2 tbsp tomato paste

1 stalk of lemon grass

½ tsp sea salt

½ tsp freshly ground pepper

1 tbsp chopped cilantro

PREPARATION

Combine the shrimp with the lime zest, juice, coriander, and ginger. Marinate for 30 minutes.

Meanwhile, heat the olive oil over medium heat; add the onion and celery and cook until lightly browned. Add all the other ingredients except the shrimp and cilantro. Bring to a boil and simmer for 20 minutes.

Remove the lemon grass; add the marinated shrimp and the cilantro. Cook for 5 minutes and serve hot.

Serves 8

These days, especially here on Mustique, there are many requests for Thai dishes, and consequently all the ingredients are readily available. This soup has proved very popular at events I've catered in both the Caribbean and Canada.

Asian marinated vegetables

Serves 8

This very
healthy salad
will impress
with both its
taste and eye
appeal.

INGREDIENTS

1 lb carrots, peeled and cut into 1½ inch pieces

1 lb English cucumbers, peeled and cut into 1½ inch pieces

1 lb celery, cut into 1½ inch pieces

1 lb green and red sweet peppers, deseeded and cut into 1½ inch pieces

Marinade:

1 tbsp chopped fresh ginger

1 tbsp chopped galanga

1½ cups peanut oil

¼ cup sesame oil

¼ cup brown rice vinegar

1 stalk of lemon grass

1½ tsp fish sauce

1½ tsp ground black pepper

1 tsp light soy sauce

PREPARATION

Combine all the marinade ingredients in a non-reactive bowl and mix together. Pour over the fresh raw vegetables. Marinate overnight and serve chilled.

Seared beef flank steak pad Thai with toasted cashews

INGREDIENTS

2 tbsp peanut or canola oil

1 lb flank steak, cut across the grain into 2 inch slices, ¼ inch thick

1 cup chopped onions

¼ cup chopped garlic

½ tsp chopped fresh lemon grass

6 Thai red chili peppers, chopped

1 red sweet pepper, deseeded and sliced

1 tsp sugar

3 tbsp fish sauce

3 tbsp fresh lime juice

2 tbsp light soy sauce

$^{1}/_{3}$ cup chopped cilantro

4 green onions, green part only, cut into 1 inch strips

1 lb packaged rice noodles, cooked as directed on package

$^{1}/_{3}$ cup coarsely chopped toasted cashews

PREPARATION

Heat a wok, add the oil, and swirl to cover the surface of the pan. Once the oil is hot, stir-fry the flank steak, and remove as soon as the meat is browned. Set aside.

In the same pan, stir-fry the onion, garlic, lemon grass, chilies, red pepper, and sugar. When lightly browned, return the beef to the pan, along with the fish sauce, lime juice, soy, cilantro, and green onions. Fold in the cooked noodles and stir for 2–3 minutes. Season with pepper, sprinkle with cashews, and serve with additional hot sauces on the side.

Serves 6

This just happens to be my favorite Thai dish.

The cooking of paella on an open fire always makes for a fun time. The color of the smells and flavors is inviting to everyone.

Spanish-style paella

INGREDIENTS

1 cup olive oil

16 chicken thighs on the bone, skin on

1 pork tenderloin, cut into ¼ inch thick pieces

4 fresh chorizo sausages, sliced

½ cup finely chopped onion

1 red or orange sweet pepper, cored, deseeded and chopped

1 tbsp chopped garlic

1 large tomato, peeled, seeded and chopped

3 cups long grain rice

1 tsp Spanish saffron

½ cup dry white wine

8 cups warm chicken stock

16 large raw shrimps in their shells

16 fresh mussels in their shells

½ cup frozen peas, defrosted

lemons, to serve

PREPARATION

Prepare the barbecue. When hot, adjust the grill so that it is approximately 3 inches away from the coals.

In a 20 inch paella pan, heat ½ cup olive oil to sear the chicken until brown on all sides. Remove to a platter. Discard the excess fat from the paella pan, add ½ cup olive oil and heat until hot. Add the pork and chorizo and brown quickly, stirring constantly. Add the onion, pepper, garlic, tomato, and rice and stir until the liquid evaporates. Add the saffron, wine, chicken stock, and sea salt and freshly ground pepper; bring up to a boil as the rice begins to expand.

Fold in the chicken pieces and the shrimp and stir thoroughly. Once the liquid starts to boil, add the remaining ingredients, arranged or scattered on top, as preferred. Allow to cook briskly for 10–12 minutes, but do not stir.

Remove from the barbecue, cover the paella with foil, and allow to rest for 5 minutes. Remove foil and serve with fresh lemons.

Serves 8

One of the highlights of my time living on Mustique was preparing this dish for a party of about 100 guests for Bud and Patsy Fisher, long-time Mustique residents. Lots of work, but a great day out! As with the national dish of any country, there are many variations on the basic paella recipe.

Arugula salad with cherry tomatoes and red onion

INGREDIENTS

6 handfuls young arugula leaves, washed

½ red onion, finely sliced

18 cherry tomatoes, halved

½ cup toasted pine nuts (optional)

Vinaigrette:

1 tsp Dijon mustard

1 tbsp balsamic vinegar

1 tsp finely chopped shallot

½ tsp sea salt

½ tsp freshly ground black pepper

5 tbsp extra virgin olive oil

PREPARATION

For the vinaigrette, combine together in a bowl the mustard, vinegar, shallot, sea salt and pepper, then slowly whisk in the olive oil until it emulsifies.

Mix the arugula, red onion, and tomatoes together. Toss with your desired quantity of vinaigrette, and sprinkle with pine nuts if desired. Transfer to a bowl and serve.

Serves 6

Pick the arugula while it is young and tender.

Makes 1 loaf

Focaccia is Italian flat bread made with olive oil, and the key to this recipe is to use the best quality fruity virgin olive oil you can find.

Focaccia bread with black and green olives

INGREDIENTS

3½ cups unbleached flour

1 tsp white sugar

1 tsp sea salt

1 tbsp active dry yeast

2 tbsp vegetable oil

1 cup water

1 egg

8 black and 8 green olives, pitted and halved

1 tsp chopped rosemary

3 tbsp virgin olive oil

PREPARATION

Mix 1 cup of the flour with the sugar, sea salt, and yeast. Warm the vegetable oil and water slightly, and add to the yeast mixture with the egg. Mix thoroughly. Fold in most of the flour, leaving a little for kneading. When thoroughly combined, knead until firm. Cover with a damp cloth and allow to prove until doubled in size (approximately 20 minutes).

Place the dough on a greased baking sheet, and roll out and shape as you desire. Cover with a damp cloth and allow to prove again for 30 minutes.

Preheat oven to 400°F.

Uncover the dough and poke holes in the surface to insert the olives. Sprinkle with the rosemary and a little sea salt. Brush with the olive oil and bake for about 20 minutes or until golden brown. Remove from the baking sheet and cool on a wire rack.

Summertime sangria with a Caribbean twist

Serves 8

INGREDIENTS

8 cups burgundy wine or good Spanish plonk

$\frac{1}{3}$ cup brandy

$\frac{1}{3}$ cup Triple Sec

2 cups orange juice

½ cup lime juice

½ cup passion fruit juice

¼ cup sugar

1 cup water

2 oranges, sliced

2 apples, sliced

1 lemon, sliced

PREPARATION

Mix all the ingredients together. Let the fruit marinate in the liquid for at least an hour, and then pour the sangria into tall glasses full of ice.

Sit back and enjoy!

Sun, sand, buckets of beer, hip music, and good company. What else is needed?

Roasted artichoke and buffalo mozzarella pizza with chili oil

Makes one 12 inch pizza

The basil and pesto really make the pizza rock.

INGREDIENTS

Dough:

1 envelope active dry yeast

1 tsp farm honey

1 cup warm (110–115°F) water

3 cups unbleached all-purpose flour

1 tsp sea salt

1 tbsp chili oil

olive oil

Topping:

1½ cups pesto sauce

16 artichoke hearts, quartered

2 cups chopped tomatoes

2 cups mozzarella, sliced

1 bunch fresh basil

hot chili oil

PREPARATION

To prepare dough, dissolve the yeast and honey in half the warm water and let stand for 5 minutes. With an electric mixer with a dough hook attachment, combine the flour and salt. Pour in the oil, and when absorbed, add the yeast mixture together with the remaining warm water. Knead on slow speed for 5 minutes. Turn out the dough onto a lightly floured surface and knead by hand for 2 minutes. The dough should be smooth and firm. Cover with a damp cloth and allow to rise in a warm area for about 30 minutes.

Work the ball of dough by pulling dough down the sides and tucking under the bottom. Repeat three to four times, then roll under the palm of your hand on an unfloured surface until smooth and firm (approximately 1 minute). Cover with a damp cloth and let rise for 30 minutes.

Preheat the oven to 500°F.

Place the ball of dough on a lightly floured surface. Press down on the center, spreading the dough by hand until desired thickness is achieved. The outer border should be a little thicker than the inner circle. Brush outer border with a little olive oil.

Prepare the topping by spreading the pesto evenly over the pizza. Arrange the artichokes in a regular fashion and add the chopped tomatoes. Top with mozzarella slices and basil leaves.

Place on a pizza stone or a baking sheet and bake in the preheated oven for 6 minutes. Remove and drizzle with hot chili oil before serving.

Makes one 12 inch pizza

Make this just before you venture to the beach, then squeeze lemon juice over the pizza before eating.

Smoked salmon, baby spinach, and Brie pizza with caper berries

INGREDIENTS

Dough:
  1 envelope active dry yeast
  1 tsp farm honey
  1 cup warm (110–115°F) water
  3 cups unbleached all-purpose flour
  1 tsp sea salt
  1 tbsp chili oil
  olive oil

Topping:
  1½ cups homemade tomato sauce
  1½ cups blanched spinach leaves
  2 small wheels of Brie, sliced
  2 cups strips of smoked salmon
  1 small red onion, sliced
  24 caper berries
  fresh dill, to garnish (optional)
  lemon halves, to serve

PREPARATION

Prepare the pizza dough as in the previous recipe.

Preheat the oven to 500°F.

Place the ball of dough on a lightly floured surface. Press down on the center, spreading the dough by hand until desired thickness is achieved. The outer border should be a little thicker than the inner circle. Brush outer border with a little olive oil.

Distribute the tomato sauce evenly over the dough and add the spinach. Add the Brie slices and top with the smoked salmon and the onion. Place on a pizza stone or a baking sheet and bake in the preheated oven for 6 minutes. Sprinkle with caper berries and garnish with fresh dill if desired.

Squeeze lemon juice on top just before eating.

Caesar salad with ciabatta croutons and shaved Parmesan

INGREDIENTS
2 garlic cloves, crushed

2 anchovy fillets, mashed

2½ tsp fresh squeezed lemon juice

1 tsp Dijon mustard

1 tsp Worcestershire sauce

½ tsp Tabasco sauce

2 large egg yolks

½ cup olive oil

2 heads Romaine lettuce, torn into bite-size pieces

½ cup shaved Parmesan cheese

bacon pieces, cooked (optional)

lemon wedges, to serve

Croutons:

3 cups day-old Italian ciabatta bread cut into ½ inch cubes

3 tbsp olive oil

3 garlic cloves, sliced

PREPARATION
Preheat the oven to 350°F.

For the croutons, combine the bread cubes with the olive oil, garlic, and some sea salt and pepper, and spread evenly on a baking sheet. Bake, turning occasionally, until golden brown. Remove from oven and drain on paper towels.

In a large wooden bowl, mash together the garlic cloves with sea salt to form a paste. Next, mash the anchovies into the garlic, and add the lemon juice, mustard, Worcestershire sauce, Tabasco, and egg yolks. Whisk well. Slowly add the olive oil, whisking constantly.

Arrange the lettuce in a salad bowl and mix with your desired amount of dressing. Toss until coated, and sprinkle in the croutons, Parmesan, and bacon if desired. Serve immediately with fresh lemon wedges.

Serves 6

Great with your favorite pizza.

The Perilous Feast

I watched a red-legged tortoise,
Whose legs aren't red at all,
Come lumbering down the terraces
Beyond our garden wall.

The sodden scree was perilous
Along those hanging tracks,
Especially for greedy-guts
With homes upon their backs.

Her scaly limbs were scrabbling
On stones as sharp as knives;
Yet on she came, oblivious,
Her eyes fixed on the prize.

So close to turning turtle,
That ancient, stubborn beast,
Risked life and limb, the ledge to win,
And there – began to feast!

Felix Dennis
Mandalay, Mustique
Christmas Eve, 2000

Thousands of red-legged tortoises roam wild on the island of Mustique. Land turtles, Mustiquans call them. This reptile's legs are covered in studs of a burnt amber or orange. They are noted for their voracious appetites, especially during breeding season when the island rings with the click-clacking of their shells as males pump furiously away for hours at a time. The females remain stationary, never ceasing to graze, outwardly oblivious of their partner's exertions!

The Callaloo...It was Emerald

When we first visited Mustique years ago, we were guests of David and Glenith Grierson, who were our neighbors in Toronto. At their lovely house, Wind Song, we enjoyed Rosyln Cruickshank's tasty callaloo soup several times.

So, when our home, Sea Fan, was finished and we had our own kitchen, I asked Roslyn how to make callaloo soup. It was simple, she said. Wash the leaves and stalks very well, chop onions and add stock!

Of course, callaloo soup can have many other additions. Ground provisions (sweet potatoes, yams, or carrots) can be added. The stock can be chicken, meat, or crab. All delicious! The soup may be served as is, or blended after it has cooled.

Well, my soup was gently bubbling away and when it turned a bright, deep green color, I turned the heat off. I'd never seen callaloo soup so appealing a green!

I decided to put the hot soup in the blender. Big mistake! The top flew off, splattering my face, neck, and dress...not to mention the walls, floor, and kitchen cabinets!

So... after a bit of a clean up, I placed the emerald green soup into bowls, and we sat down to enjoy it.

"What a delicious soup!" said Bud, clearing his throat.

"Yes, it is lovely!" I said, giving a little cough and clearing my throat...

Cough! Cough! Tickle! Tickle!

We looked at each other in surprise.

"I feel as though my throat is closing up," said Bud.

"Me, too! I can hardly swallow!"

"Quick! Quick! Drink some wine, water, anything, whatever... should we call the doctor?"

"No, it's too late in the evening! Keep drinking... I think I can swallow a little now."

So eventually we set the soup aside, caught our breath, and had a bit of our dinner... and wondered what on earth had happened.

The next day when I asked Roslyn what I'd done wrong, she said that I should have cooked the callaloo way, way longer, or thoroughly cleaned the stalks, which have tiny, tiny hairs that can cause your throat to constrict!

We've had many a callaloo soup since, but we always cook it a looooong, looooong time!

Patsy Fisher

From the Local Pot

CHAPTER SIX

From the Local Pot:
Soups from Mustique's Favorite Cooks

Being a huge fan of soup – warm, cold, chilled, vegetarian, or rich with seafood or meats – the tastes and possibilities are always enticing to me. I often judge a restaurant by the caliber of their offerings, and typically find that if the soup is not good, most often neither is the rest of the meal.

My time spent in Mustique's kitchens has been very rewarding, teaching and learning from our island's best cooks. Occasionally I was met with a bit of suspicion in the beginning, but mostly was welcomed with great warmth. A cook's domain is a sacred arena, a territory to tread carefully in, and always something to respect. The various preparations and styles of these soups, broths, bisques, consommés, and chowders cover the range of my most favorite flavors – made all the more special because the recipes here were created by Mustique's very own best cooks.

Recipes

Callaloo soup | West Indian boilene | Spicy tomato and lentil
Chicken coconut broth with sweet corn and lemon grass | Christophene with garden chives
Plantain soup | Chilled cucumber | Creamed carrot soup | Lobster bisque
Pumpkin soup | Coconut curried vegetable soup
Chilled cucumber soup with dill and cucumber sorbet | Roasted red pepper and coconut broth with Thai spice
Watercress and toasted almond soup with crème fraîche

Callaloo soup

by Eversley Webb

This is a classic Creole dish, made all the more unique by each cook creating their very own special interpretation. This soup is truly a staple on Mustique, served by every home – by the Cotton House and Firefly as well – and it is surprising how different each bowl can taste. You will also discover in your travels that there are alternative spellings in different regions of the world: calaloo, callilu, and callaloo.

Essentially, callaloo are the young leaves from the eddoe or dasheen plant, quite similar to spinach in the rest of the world.

INGREDIENTS

4 bundles callaloo

2 tannia, peeled

8 cups chicken stock

¼ cup chopped onion

2 garlic cloves, chopped

4 sweet peppers, chopped

PREPARATION

Wash the callaloo and chop. Dice the tannia finely and add with the callaloo to the chicken stock in a soup pot. Add the rest of the ingredients, bring to a boil, and let boil for 30 minutes. Reduce the heat and allow to simmer for another 15 minutes. Add sea salt and pepper to taste. Cool to room temperature then process in a food processor.

Serve hot.

Serves 6

West Indian boilene

by Eversley Webb

This is a typical dish of St. Vincent, with the main ingredient being fish. Pick whatever is freshest at the fish market, and explore the variations.

INGREDIENTS

2 lb fresh fish

2 tbsp green seasoning (see page 70)

1 lb eddoes

4 green bananas

1 lb potatoes

2 carrots

1 cup chopped green onion

2 garlic cloves

2 leaves of ticky thyme or ordinary thyme

1 flavor pepper (hot pepper)

4 cups water

juice of 1 lime

PREPARATION

Clean the fish and marinate in the green seasoning. Peel all the vegetables and roots, and dice.

Place the prepared vegetables and the green onion, garlic, thyme, and pepper in a large pot with the water and bring to a boil. When the vegetables are nearly cooked and the stock has reduced by half, place the fish on top of the vegetables. Do not stir, just shake the pot from side to side. Add lime juice to taste, together with sea salt and pepper. When the vegetables are cooked, the soup is ready to serve.

Serves 6

EVERSLEY WEBB is a strong family man of great warmth and is also a good friend. After working at the Cotton House and then for Mr. David Bowie, these last few years "Webb" has settled at the home of Mr. Felix Dennis of Dennis Publishing. At Felix's house, Mandalay, as Webb's cooking continues to evolve, his creative talents keep the guests very happy.

WEST INDIAN BOILENE

ROLAND CATO, a man of many talents, spent seven years working in neighboring Canaoun. He brings to Alumbrera a multitude of different culinary styles.

SPICY TOMATO AND LENTIL

Spicy tomato and lentil
by Roland Cato

This wonderful combination produces total harmony with a spicy edge.

INGREDIENTS
2 tbsp sunflower oil

2 onions, finely chopped

4 garlic cloves, crushed

3 tbsp finely chopped fresh ginger

2 tsp cumin seeds, crushed

2 lb ripe tomatoes, peeled, deseeded and chopped

1 cup lentils

10 cups vegetable or chicken stock

2 tbsp tomato paste

low-fat yogurt and chopped fresh parsley, to garnish

PREPARATION
Heat the sunflower oil in a large heavy-based saucepan and cook the chopped onion gently for 5 minutes until softened. Stir in the garlic, ginger, and cumin followed by the tomatoes and lentils. Cook over low heat for 3–4 minutes. Stir in the stock and tomato paste. Bring to a boil, then lower the heat. Simmer gently for about 30 minutes until the lentils are soft. Season with sea salt and pepper.

Puree the soup in a blender or food processor. Return to the clean pan and reheat slowly. Garnish each portion with yogurt and a little chopped parsley.

Serves 8

Chicken coconut broth with sweet corn and lemon grass
by Roland Cato

Always a superb marriage – coconut and lemon grass are the perfect pair.

INGREDIENTS
6 cups coconut milk

4 cups chicken stock

8 stalks of lemon grass, bruised and chopped

20 peppercorns, crushed

10 lime leaves, torn

1¾ lb boneless chicken, cut into thin strips

8 oz button mushrooms

4 oz baby sweet corn

8 tbsp lime juice

6 tbsp fish sauce

4 fresh chilies, seeded and chopped

chopped green onions and cilantro leaves, to garnish

PREPARATION
Bring the coconut milk and chicken stock to a boil. Add the lemon grass, peppercorns, and 5 lime leaves. Reduce the heat and simmer gently for 10 minutes. Strain the stock into a clean pan. Over low heat, add the chicken, button mushrooms, and baby corn to the stock. Simmer for 5–7 minutes or until the chicken is cooked. Stir in the lime juice, fish sauce, and the rest of the lime leaves. Serve hot, sprinkled with chopped chilies and garnished with green onions and cilantro.

Serves 12

Christophene with garden chives

by Michael Charles

Chayote is another name for this tropical squash, which originated in Mexico but is now available throughout the West Indies.

INGREDIENTS

6 large christophenes

2 onions, chopped

3 garlic cloves, chopped

$\frac{1}{3}$ cup olive oil

6 cups chicken stock

3 celery leaves

3 parsley leaves

fresh chives, chopped

whipped heavy cream, to garnish

PREPARATION

Peel, wash and cut the christophenes into cubes. In a large pan sauté the christophenes, onion, and garlic in the olive oil for about 20 minutes. Add the chicken stock and cook for about 8 minutes. Blend in a processor or blender with the celery and parsley. Add sea salt and pepper to taste.

Serve hot or cold, sprinkled with fresh chives, with a dollop of whipped heavy cream as a garnish.

Serves 6

Plantain soup

by Michael Charles

An unlikely candidate for a soup and a close relative to the banana, plantains, which are technically a fruit, are mostly used as a vegetable. Very flavorful – as well as a good conversation piece for your table!

INGREDIENTS

4 large ripe plantains

7 cups chicken stock

2 onions, chopped

2 garlic cloves, chopped

1 large bell pepper, chopped

plantain slices, fried, to garnish

PREPARATION

Peel and remove the black insides of the plantains. Cut into cubes. Cook in the chicken stock for 15 minutes together with the onion, garlic, and bell pepper. Add sea salt and pepper to taste. Blend in a food processor or blender and serve hot.

Garnish with fried plantain slices.

Serves 6

MICHAEL CHARLES
(Josh to his friends)
spent 11 years at
Discovery House and
is now at Callaloo,
specializing in West
Indian food. Josh is
also the creator of
Grenadines Crunch,
a new granola product
we all enjoy every day
on Mustique.

CHRISTOPHENE WITH GARDEN CHIVES

BEVAN WILKES works at one of Mustique's most popular homes, L'Ansecoy, where she has been perfecting and honing her skills for the past seven years. During this time, her training has taken her to New York's finest seafood restaurant, Le Bernardin, a privilege extended by the owner.

CREAMED CARROT SOUP

Chilled cucumber

by Bevan Wilkes

Refreshingly good!

INGREDIENTS

4 large cucumbers, peeled and seeded

1 cup crème fraîche

1 cup heavy cream

½ cup finely grated Parmesan cheese

2 garlic cloves, minced

1 tsp Tabasco sauce

juice of ½ lemon

PREPARATION

Using an electric juicer, juice the cucumbers. Press the juice and pulp mixture through a fine-mesh sieve into a bowl. You should have 5 cups cucumber juice. Add the crème fraîche, heavy cream, Parmesan cheese, garlic, and Tabasco. Place the soup in the refrigerator for 2 hours to marry the flavors.

To serve, strain the soup through a fine-mesh sieve. Season with fine sea salt and freshly ground white pepper to taste. Squeeze the lemon juice into the soup and ladle into chilled bowls.

Serves 8

Creamed carrot soup

by Bevan Wilkes

For an added element, add a teaspoon of freshly chopped ginger while cooking.

INGREDIENTS

2 tbsp unsalted butter

½ onion, chopped

1 tsp chopped garlic

6 carrots, peeled and sliced

3 cups chicken stock

¼ cup heavy cream

PREPARATION

In a medium saucepan over medium heat, melt the butter. Add the onion and garlic and sauté for 2 minutes – do not allow to burn. Add the sliced carrots and 1 cup of the chicken stock, stir and allow to cook for 3 minutes. Turn up the heat and add the remaining 2 cups chicken stock. Add fine sea salt and freshly ground black pepper to taste and cook for 5 minutes.

Remove from the heat and set aside to cool. Pour into a blender and blend until smooth. Transfer to a saucepan and reheat over medium heat. Stir in the heavy cream and do not allow to boil. Pour into warmed bowls and serve immediately.

Serves 8

Lobster bisque

by Augustine John

"Give me more, give me more!" was my first feeling after tasting this colorful treat.

INGREDIENTS

1 onion, chopped

2 stalks of celery, chopped

1 fresh bay leaf

3 large garlic cloves

8 oz shrimp shells

1 lobster head, chopped and cleaned

1 tbsp olive oil

1 tbsp fresh thyme

4 cups water

1 cup fish stock

2 tsp paprika

1 cup heavy cream

1 cup tomato paste

1 tsp sea salt

¼ tsp white pepper

cornstarch (optional)

1 tbsp chopped chives, to garnish

PREPARATION

In a heavy-based saucepan, add the onion, celery, bay leaf, garlic, shrimp shells, lobster head, olive oil, and thyme and sauté until all are seared. Add the water and bring to a boil for 20 minutes. Remove the pan from the heat and strain into a clean pot.

Add the fish stock, paprika, cream, tomato paste, sea salt, and pepper and bring to a boil over medium heat. Adjust seasoning to taste, thickening with cornstarch, if desired. Serve hot, garnished with chopped chives.

Serves 6

Pumpkin soup

by Augustine John

A local favorite – any time of the year!

INGREDIENTS

1 medium pumpkin, peeled and chopped

1 small onion, chopped

1 garlic clove

1 stalk of celery

3 cups water

¼ tsp sea salt

1 cup chicken stock

½ cup heavy cream

¼ cup sour cream or ½ cup toasted pumpkin seeds, to garnish

PREPARATION

In a medium saucepan, bring all the ingredients except the cream to a boil for 15 minutes. Remove from the heat and blend until smooth. Return to the heat and season to taste. Add cream and cook over low heat for 10 minutes.

Serve hot, garnished with a dollop of sour cream or sprinkled with toasted pumpkin seeds.

Serves 8

PUMPKIN SOUP

Her Style was in Her Grace

Mustique is a land of legends, possibly more than almost any other place on earth. It is, in many ways, a Never-Never Land all its own. That is why, I think, only those with a very special love in their hearts and a peace of spirit are drawn here.

HRH Princess Margaret was one of the most special.

I recall her as a high-spirited and unique person who left no doubt of her royal heritage. Still, there was a wonderful humanity to Princess Margaret, and many of us were privileged to have called her "friend."

In 1995, Alex Beard, son of Pat Beard and nephew of photographer Peter Beard, came to stay in Mustique. A young man in his mid-twenties, he was trying to "find" his artistic self. A hedonist since birth, and inspired by the stories of his scandalous uncle, he sought to make a similar mark for himself. Pat sent him to me so we could bond, and Alex could paint. For several months, Alex assumed his best Robinson Crusoe stance, and, brush in hand, he created drawings of trees with snakes for leaves, dogs with human skulls as eyeballs, and pointy figures of humans with tongues extended meters beyond their heads, where they embraced alligators and more skulls. He had "found himself," but no one was sure who the "he" was he had found, and least of all, Princess Margaret.

The Princess was hosting a luncheon, and Alex attended. As HRH knew members of the Beard clan, she was interested in his art. It was hung in "exhibition" at the bar, and arrangements were made for Princess Margaret to view his work. She arrived at sunset as planned, and made her way around the bar, carefully examining each piece. On her return to the table, she looked at Alex, who was a-flutter in anticipation. She drew herself up, looked him square in the eye, and said, "How can such a nice young man as you create such horrible things?"

There was no reply, there could be none, and neither Alex nor I ever forgot the Princess who was not afraid to speak the truth. She had said what everyone else was reluctant to ask. It took some time, but today, Alex has found himself, a beautiful and talented wife, and his artistic voice. His work is unusual, and absent are the snakes, skulls, and alligators of those dark days, and for that we are all very glad.

And to Princess Margaret, know that we all miss you very much.

One love,
Basil

FORNESTA C. HAZELL was born in St. Vincent and trained under a well-known chef from the Bahamas. She brings with her to Toucan Hill a blend of Caribbean and international cuisine and is stylish as well as contemporary in her cooking.

CHILLED CUCUMBER SOUP WITH DILL AND CUCUMBER SORBET

Coconut curried vegetable soup
by Fornesta C. Hazell

Your vegetarian friends will love this wonderful soup as a starter, or as a meal in itself served with a fresh green salad and warm bread.

INGREDIENTS
2 tbsp vegetable oil

6 garlic cloves, chopped

2 onions, chopped

2 heaping tbsp curry powder

2 tsp ground coriander

2 tsp ground cumin

2 cups fresh coconut milk

1½ cups carrots, cut into 1 inch cubes

1 cup zucchini, cut into 1 inch cubes

2 cups red sweet pepper, cut into 1 inch cubes

2 cups green sweet pepper, cut into 1 inch cubes

4 cups vegetable stock

plain yogurt or cream

roasted shredded coconut, to garnish

PREPARATION
Heat the oil in a saucepan over medium heat. Add the garlic and onion and sauté until fragrant. Add the curry powder, coriander, cumin, and coconut milk. Cook for 1 minute. Add all the vegetables and stir to coat with the spices. Add the vegetable stock and sea salt to taste. Bring to a boil, cover, and simmer for 45 minutes over low heat.

Serve drizzled with yogurt or cream and garnished with roasted coconut.

Serves 6

Chilled cucumber soup with dill and cucumber sorbet
by Fornesta C. Hazell

Definitely one to please your guests in both taste and eye-appeal. The spice of the sorbet combines with the delicate flavor of the cucumber.

INGREDIENTS
9 cucumbers, peeled and seeds removed

1 small onion, chopped

2 garlic cloves, minced

2½ cups chicken stock

1½ cups plain yogurt

1 tbsp chopped mint

½ tsp lemon juice

mint or dill leaves, to garnish

Sorbet:

4 cucumbers

grated zest of 2 limes

1 cup fresh dill

1²/₃ cups sugar syrup

½ tsp hot sauce

4 heaping tsp yogurt

sea salt and pepper, to taste

PREPARATION
For the sorbet, blend all the ingredients in a blender until smooth. Chill in the refrigerator for a minimum of 2 hours then process in an ice-cream maker or place in ice-cube trays and freeze.

Cut eight of the cucumbers into 1 inch pieces. Combine the cucumber, onion, and garlic in a food processor or blender. Blend until smooth. Add the chicken stock, yogurt, mint, and lemon juice. Blend to combine. Add sea salt and pepper to taste. Cover and chill.

To serve, shred the remaining cucumber. Place a tablespoon of shredded cucumber in the center of a soup bowl. Add a scoop of the sorbet on top of the cucumber. Pour soup into the bowl to cover the shredded cucumber. Garnish the sorbet with a fresh mint or dill leaf.

Serves 8

Roasted red pepper and coconut broth with Thai spice

by Kevin Snook

Another great combination with that added twist of Thai curry paste.

INGREDIENTS

2 tbsp vegetable oil or butter

2 onions, coarsely chopped

2 garlic cloves

2 small tins red pimentos, chopped (1 tbsp reserved, to garnish)

2 ripe tomatoes, coarsely chopped

2 tbsp chopped parsley

2 tbsp chopped celery

6 cups vegetable stock

1 cup coconut milk

½ tsp red Thai curry paste

½ tsp honey

1 tsp chili oil

chopped green onion, to garnish

PREPARATION

Heat the oil in a large pan and add the onions, garlic, and red pimentos. Sauté until lightly brown. Add the chopped tomatoes, parsley, and celery and cook for 3–4 minutes. Add all the other ingredients. Bring to a boil and simmer gently for 30 minutes.

Strain the broth through a metal sieve into a serving bowl and season with sea salt and pepper to taste. Drizzle chili oil on the surface and garnish with chopped pimentos and green onion.

Serves 8

Watercress and toasted almond soup with crème fraîche

by Kevin Snook

They say one lives longer on a diet of watercress – with a natural abundance of iron!

INGREDIENTS

3 tbsp unsalted butter

1 cup finely chopped onion

1½ cups diced potatoes

4 cups mild chicken or vegetable stock

4 bunches of watercress, chopped

½ bunch of parsley

8 tsp crème fraîche

½ cup toasted slivered almonds

PREPARATION

Melt the butter in a saucepan. Add the onion and potatoes and sauté for a few minutes while stirring. Add the stock to the mixture, bring to a boil and let it simmer. When the potatoes and onions are soft, add the watercress and parsley. Boil, uncovered, for 2–3 minutes so that the soup retains its green color.

Puree the soup in a blender and season to taste with sea salt and black pepper. Ladle the soup into soup bowls. Add a dollop of crème fraîche to each bowl and sprinkle with toasted almonds.

Serves 8

WATERCRESS AND TOASTED ALMOND SOUP WITH CRÈME FRAÎCHE

Sunset Serenade

CHAPTER SEVEN

Sunset Serenade: Cocktails and Canapés

The island of Mustique often brings us a sunset horizon of technicolored skies…the search for the elusive "green flash" setting the mood for those who live or visit here to enjoy a "sundowner" cocktail with our friends, setting the mood for many of us who live here to indulge…yes, that's right!

Cocktail hour – time to chill, time to hang, time to relax from a busy (or not so busy) schedule – where

seven

fresh tropical drinks are accompanied by nibbles and goodies. I've been fortunate enough to have attended and catered many cocktail parties and other gatherings.

Here are some samples of a few dishes I've created, as well as some specialty drinks contributed by my good friends Patrick Klone, head bartender for nearly a decade at Firefly, and Jenson Lynch, butler at Blackstone House.

Recipes

Endeavor cocktail | Sundance cocktail | Tropical breeze | Hibiscus tea martini

Cotton tail | Mustique fun | Plantain chips with guacamole | Spicy lentil cakes with tomato relish

Sweet potato chips with arugula pesto | Herbed pita chips with eggplant, chick pea, and red pepper dips

Spicy nuts | Marinated citrus olives | Bacon-wrapped plantain with dried figs

Tri-tri ackra | Grilled chicken satay with peanut sauce | Coconut chips with sea salt

Endeavor cocktail
by Patrick Klone

Serves 1

INGREDIENTS

1 oz white rum

1 oz Amaretto

2 oz orange juice

½ ripe banana

coconut cream, to taste

ice

PREPARATION

Combine all the ingredients together. Blend and serve.

Sundance cocktail

Serves 1

INGREDIENTS

2 oz dark rum

1 oz pineapple juice

1 oz orange juice

splash of grenadine syrup

½ ripe banana

coconut cream, to taste

ice

Also created by Patrick Klone, for one of Mustique's homeowners.

PREPARATION

Combine all the ingredients together. Blend and serve.

Tropical breeze

INGREDIENTS

$^1/_3$ oz Malibu rum

½ oz peach schnapps

½ oz citrus vodka

3 oz freshly squeezed orange juice

½ oz cranberry juice

PREPARATION

Combine all the ingredients together. Serve in a tall glass filled with ice.

Serves 1

Refreshing, cool, and light.

Hibiscus tea martini

INGREDIENTS

½ oz orange vodka

½ oz Tangerine Sourpuss

2 oz fresh orange juice

1 oz hibiscus infused tea (use dried hibiscus flowers)

½ oz sugar syrup

PREPARATION

Fill your martini shaker with ice and add all the ingredients. Shake well and strain into an iced martini glass.

Serves 1

I'm always in search of anything different, especially when it's good. This is a variation of a drink I enjoyed when last in Vancouver.

Cotton tail

by Jenson Lynch

Serves 1

This one's
always popular
with the girls.

INGREDIENTS

1 oz white rum

1 oz dark rum

½ oz Malibu rum

1½ oz coconut cream

3 oz pineapple juice

½ fresh mango

½ cup ice

cherry or mango slice, to garnish

PREPARATION

Combine all the ingredients in a blender. Blend until smooth. Serve cold and garnish with a slice of mango or a cherry.

Mustique fun

Serves 1

This is another
Jenson favorite.

INGREDIENTS

1 oz white rum

1 oz dark rum

½ oz Amaretto

½ oz grenadine syrup

¼ oz lime juice

4 oz cranberry juice

apple slice or cherry, to garnish

PREPARATION

Fill a shaker half way with ice. Combine all the ingredients in the shaker and shake. Pour into a glass three quarters filled with ice. Garnish with an apple slice or cherry and serve.

Plantain chips with guacamole

INGREDIENTS

6 large green plantains

vegetable oil for deep-frying

Guacamole:

5 ripe avocados, mashed

juice of 1 lime

½ cup diced tomato

½ cup diced red onion

1 tbsp chopped garlic

2 tbsp chopped cilantro

1 tsp hot sauce

PREPARATION

Peel the plantains under running water to avoid staining your hands. Cut lengthwise into ⅛ inch thick slices. Heat vegetable oil to 350°F and then drop the plantain slices into the oil a few at a time and fry until crispy. Drain on paper towels. When all the chips are done, sprinkle with sea salt and serve.

For the guacamole, mix all the ingredients together; add sea salt and pepper to taste.

Serves 8

A member of the banana family but more starchy, plantains are never eaten raw but make an ideal accompaniment to pre-dinner drinks when prepared like this.

Spicy lentil cakes with tomato relish

INGREDIENTS

peanut oil for frying

2 onions, finely chopped

1 stalk of celery, finely chopped

1 carrot, finely chopped

1 garlic clove, finely chopped

2 cups cooked brown lentils (well drained)

1 tbsp olive oil

1 egg yolk

3 tbsp breadcrumbs

½ tbsp ground cumin

½ tbsp ground coriander

6 tbsp chopped parsley

1 tbsp chopped cilantro

1 tsp lemon juice

flour for dredging

Relish:

1 onion, sliced

12 small plum tomatoes, coarsely chopped

1 tbsp sugar

1 tbsp white vinegar

sea salt and pepper

PREPARATION

For the tomato relish, combine all the ingredients in a pan over low heat and simmer until most of the liquid has evaporated.

Heat some peanut oil in a skillet and cook the onion, celery, carrot, and garlic until slightly brown. Remove from the pan with a slotted spoon and place in a large bowl. Add all the other ingredients and combine well. Form into cakes of the desired size and dredge with flour.

Cook in the heated oil and turn over when lightly browned. Place on paper towel to drain. Transfer to a serving dish and accompany with the warm tomato relish.

Serves 12

A hint of Morocco, this is excellent served warm, with a sublime touch of tomato relish.

Sweet potato chips
with arugula pesto

Serves 6–8

This peppery green herb is a favorite in salads. On occasion, I'll find it fresh-grown by one of my farmers in St. Vincent and I'll grab it up for this special dish.

INGREDIENTS

6 sweet potatoes or yams

2 tbsp peanut oil

hot sauce

Pesto:

1¼ cups arugula leaves

3 garlic cloves

1 tsp sea salt

¼ cup pine nuts

¼ cup grated Parmesan cheese

¼ cup extra virgin olive oil

PREPARATION

For the pesto, place the arugula and garlic in a food processor. Pulse well to chop. Add the sea salt, pine nuts, Parmesan, and olive oil and pulse to mix. Season as needed.

Preheat oven to 375°F.

Cut the peeled sweet potatoes into wedges. Brush with the peanut oil and sprinkle with hot sauce. Place on a baking sheet and bake in the oven until crisp and tender, about 20 minutes. Serve hot with the pesto.

Herbed pita chips with eggplant, chickpea, and red pepper dips

INGREDIENTS
2 garlic cloves, finely chopped

6 tbsp olive oil

4 whole-wheat pita breads

1 tbsp thyme leaves

1 tbsp dried oregano

¼ tsp paprika

PREPARATION
Preheat oven to 350°F.

Stir the garlic into the oil. Cut the pita breads into even strips and separate. Place the pita slices split side up on a baking sheet and brush with the garlic oil. Sprinkle with the thyme, oregano, and paprika. Bake until golden brown, cool and serve with dips.

Serves 8

Three totally different tastes to enhance your party.

Chickpea dip
INGREDIENTS
2 cups chickpeas, cooked

2 garlic cloves

juice of 1½ lemons

3 tbsp olive oil

3 tbsp tahini

1 tbsp ground cumin

extra virgin olive oil, to garnish

PREPARATION
Place the chickpeas, garlic, lemon juice, olive oil, tahini, and cumin in a food processor and blend until a paste forms. Add water until smooth and creamy. Season with sea salt and pepper to taste. Turn into a bowl and drizzle with extra virgin olive oil.

Eggplant dip
INGREDIENTS
1 large eggplant

2 garlic cloves

2 tbsp tahini

1 tbsp olive oil

sea salt and pepper

juice of 1 lemon

parsley

PREPARATION
Preheat the oven to 425°F.

Bake the eggplant until brown on the outside and the flesh is soft. Scoop the flesh into a food processor and add all the other ingredients. Blend until smooth.

Roasted red pepper dip
INGREDIENTS
3 roasted red sweet peppers, peeled and deseeded

1½ cups feta cheese

4 oz cream cheese

1 garlic clove

3 tbsp fresh mint leaves

⅓ cup olive oil

1 tbsp lemon juice

PREPARATION
Place the peppers, feta cheese, cream cheese, garlic, mint, olive oil, and lemon juice in a food processor. Pulse until blended but still with some texture. If necessary add a little water. Season with sea salt and black pepper, chill and serve.

Spicy nuts

INGREDIENTS

1 cup whole blanched almonds

1 cup pecan halves

1 cup blanched and peeled hazelnuts

1 tbsp peanut oil

2 tbsp sugar

1 tsp sea salt

½ tsp cayenne pepper

½ tsp ground cumin

PREPARATION

Preheat oven to 325°F.

Roast the nuts on a baking sheet for 20 minutes, shaking periodically.

Heat the oil over medium heat and add the nuts, sugar, and sea salt. Cook until the sugar starts to caramelize slightly. Pour into a bowl and toss with the cayenne, cumin, and more sea salt to taste. Serve at room temperature.

Serves 8–10

These make a great accompaniment for martinis or a crisp glass of beer.

Marinated citrus olives

INGREDIENTS

4 tbsp olive oil

1 small onion, coarsely chopped

2 garlic cloves, chopped

1 tsp fennel seeds

2 cups mixed Greek, green and black olives, drained

1 tsp chopped rosemary

1 tsp orange zest

2 tsp crushed red pepper flakes

1 tbsp lemon juice

PREPARATION

Heat the olive oil over medium heat and add the onion, garlic, and fennel seeds. Allow to partially cook, then add the balance of the ingredients and heat through. Let marinate for 4 hours. Warm when ready to serve.

Serves 8–10

Definitely one of my most requested party favorites, best served warm.

Take Me There

My first trip to Mustique, although not one I can remember, finds its way to my thoughts often. I was a baby, a mere ten days old, and I was traveling to Mustique with my family, after news that my grandfather, Russell Penniman, had died. Russell had resided in Mustique for many years, and had just returned to his home, Cocoa Palm Beach, after visiting me, his daughter's first child.

Although the island has bittersweet memories of a great man I never knew, I find myself wanting to go back all the time to the welcoming and warm persona that it possesses. To wake to exotic birds singing, eating picnics along white sand beaches with glassy aqua water. A place where shoes are optional and having a good time is a requirement. Sitting at Basil's Bar and sipping my delicious smoothie are my most valued moments of the entire year. With legs on the table, slouched in my oversized, comfy bamboo chair, I watch for the infamous "green flash" at sunset. And although I have never actually seen the flash just as the fluorescent orange sun teases its beauty seconds before darkness, I enjoy the serenity and the tradition of waiting. I stare in calmness, surrounded by people that are doing the same thing as I, people that I love — my family, people of the island, homeowners I have never been acquainted with. But I still love them.

We meet people over the years, people that become acquaintances, friends, or lifelong soulmates. We meet them in school, through friends, family, a childhood neighbor, through the events of life and living. Mustique friends are in a category all their own. These people are special. Whether you met them at the Cotton House cocktail party on Tuesday night or at Macaroni Beach picnic when you shared your table, you forever have them in your heart. They are good people, and you are lucky if you are ever graced with the pleasure of meeting these Mustique friends.

One Mustique friend I will never forget is my grandfather. As I visit the bench placed in his memory on L'Ansecoy Bay, I can just be there ... and being there helps me fill the void of never knowing him. Sitting on the bench and climbing the rocks next to it, it comforts me to be in the last place where he was. Jealous that the ocean was the one that kissed him away, and not me. Handprints set on the back of the bench recognize the ones who loved him most, but footprints of those who visit the island and love it most will forever leave an impression on the white sand beaches. Although my heart is filled with some sadness every time the thought of him is in my head, I am content knowing the magical island of Mustique was the last place he was.

I am now only 15 and I wish to live on the wondrous island one day. I want to enjoy great meals with amazing friends and many laughs – the closest I can get to my grandfather sitting there with me at the party. That's the kind of person he was, and the person I would like to be, an amazing soul and one to make great memories for the people around him. And only one mystical, perfect place can allow me to realize who he was and celebrate the years to come . . . Mustique.

Caroline Meriwether Schmidt

Bacon-wrapped plantain with dried figs

INGREDIENTS

10 slices smoked bacon, cut in half

10 dried figs, cut in half

1 plantain, cut into ¼ inch slices, then in half

PREPARATION

Preheat oven to 375°F. Presoak 20 toothpicks in cold water.

Flatten each piece of bacon with a heavy knife to prevent shrinkage when cooking. Place each fig on a plantain slice and wrap together with the bacon. Secure with a toothpick. Put on baking tray and bake until crisp, about 12 minutes. Serve warm.

Makes 20

A crunchy and moist tasty treat.

Tri-tri ackra

INGREDIENTS
vegetable oil for pan-frying

2 cups tri-tri, washed and drained

1 egg, beaten

1 green onion, chopped

¼ tsp ground cloves

2 garlic cloves, chopped

2 red hot peppers, deseeded and chopped

1½ cups flour

sea salt and pepper, to taste

PREPARATION
Preheat the oil in a skillet.

Mix all the remaining ingredients together thoroughly. Drop teaspoon-sized dollops of mixture into the heated oil. When golden brown on all sides, remove, drain on paper towels and enjoy.

Serves 6

Certainly a delicacy and a real treat, these miniature river fish are found only during certain times of the year in the unpolluted rivers of St. Vincent.

Grilled chicken satay with peanut sauce

Serves 12

A touch of Thailand and always a crowd pleaser.

INGREDIENTS

6 boneless chicken breasts, cut into strips

Marinade:

2 tbsp curry powder

1½ tsp honey

½ tsp sea salt

1½ tsp rice vinegar

¾ cup coconut milk

Peanut sauce:

¼ cup vegetable oil

1 tsp curry paste

1 tsp chili paste

1 tsp paprika

1 cup coconut milk

1 cup unsalted peanuts, finely ground

¼ cup chicken stock

¼ cup fish sauce

¼ cup honey

2 tbsp lime juice

PREPARATION

Presoak twelve 6 inch bamboo skewers in water for 2 hours.

Skewer the chicken strips. Whisk together the marinade ingredients and marinate the chicken skewers for 4 hours in the refrigerator. Bring to room temperature before cooking.

For the peanut sauce, heat the vegetable oil and add the curry paste, chili paste, paprika, a third of the coconut milk, the peanuts, chicken stock, fish sauce, honey, and lime juice. Bring to a boil, stirring constantly. When reduced by half, add the remaining coconut milk, return to a boil, and simmer for 20 minutes. Set aside until needed.

Remove the chicken from the marinade. Grill the chicken skewers for 2–3 minutes on each side and serve with the peanut sauce.

Coconut chips
with sea salt

INGREDIENTS

1 coconut

butter

sea salt

PREPARATION

Preheat oven to 375°F, and prepare a baking sheet by rubbing with butter.

Break open the coconut, and remove the meat from the shell using a sharp vegetable peeler. Shave the coconut into thin slices.

Arrange the coconut slices on the prepared baking sheet and bake for 10–12 minutes until light golden brown, turning occasionally. Sprinkle with sea salt, and serve in an empty coconut shell.

Always a bar snack at cocktail hour in the Firefly – this is my take on these scrumptious treats.

On Checkered Cloth

CHAPTER EIGHT

On Checkered Cloth:
A Picnic Here, a Picnic There

eight

A picnic can be a celebration of a special occasion, a time to relax, a moment to enjoy and appreciate the world around us. Finding that ideal location can sometimes be a challenge…but excursions up to the hills, secluded romantic beaches, and hidden pathways to secret spots are all part of the fun. And if all the preparation is done ahead of time, then your only task is to keep your eyes peeled for the perfect place to pitch the checkered cloth.

Here is a small sampling of favorite recipes to try.

Recipes

Caribbean roti | Spicy coleslaw | Room-temperature pasta salad

Mustard and garlic roasted beef tenderloin with watercress | Seared pork and eggplant panini

Toasted baguettes with oven-roasted tomatoes, garlic, and basil | Leek, onion, and cheese tart

Kevin's Caribbean fried chicken | Mango Caribbean champagne | Spiced iced tea

Caribbean roti

INGREDIENTS

Dough:

2 lb all-purpose flour

1 tbsp yeast (follow package instructions to activate yeast)

pinch of goya all-purpose seasoning

1 tbsp curry powder

½ cup melted butter

½ cup melted lard

Filling:

unsalted butter

chopped onions

chopped garlic

curry powder

water or chicken stock, with equal amount of cream

cooked chicken, beef, shrimp, or veggies

PREPARATION

Mix all the ingredients for the dough together. Knead well and leave to rise until doubled in size. Divide into balls about the size of a small orange. Roll out each ball into a flat pancake.

Meanwhile, prepare the filling. Melt some butter, and add chopped onion, garlic, and curry powder. Gently fry until all are golden in color. Add equal quantities of water or stock and cream and continue cooking until a smooth thick sauce is formed. Add your desired filling ingredient and heat through. Allow to cool.

Using a well-greased and hot roti pan, place the dough cakes one at a time into the pan and allow to cook. Brush with vegetable oil and turn over until the roti is cooked but still soft.

Put the filling inside the roti. Fold and wrap in foil to keep warm.

NOTE

As you can see, there are no specific quantities for the filling, so use your free spirit and add as you desire.

Serves 16

This recipe was kindly given to me by Elizabeth Clayton, the gracious host and owner of the very popular Firefly. Many a lunchtime, I've indulged in this tasty Caribbean classic. Authentically from Trinidad, where the dough would be made with ground cooked split peas, or dhali would be folded into the finished dough and rolled out. This dish is further complemented by a spicy mango chutney.

Serves 8

A great summer salad. The addition of corn gives it a wonderful sweetness to complement the hint of heat.

Spicy coleslaw

INGREDIENTS

1 cup mayonnaise

1 tbsp lime juice

1 tbsp ground cumin

1 tsp cayenne pepper

1 tsp sea salt

1 tsp ground black pepper

1 large carrot, peeled and grated

2 radishes, thinly sliced

1 cup chopped fresh pineapple

1 head green cabbage, washed and thinly sliced

1 cup sweet corn (optional)

PREPARATION

In a stainless-steel bowl, stir together all the ingredients. Combine well; allow to sit for 45 minutes before serving.

Room-temperature pasta salad

INGREDIENTS

1 lb bowtie pasta, cooked al dente and drained

1 cup bite-size broccoli pieces, lightly blanched

1 cup bite-size cauliflower pieces, lightly blanched

1 cup bite-size zucchini pieces, lightly blanched

½ cup cherry tomatoes

⅓ cup each sliced red, yellow, and green sweet peppers

2 garlic cloves, finely chopped

2 tbsp chopped parsley

2 tbsp fresh basil

1 cup of your favorite vinaigrette

PREPARATION

In a stainless-steel bowl, mix the pasta and vegetables. Toss together with the vinaigrette. Add sea salt and black pepper to taste.

Serves 8

Colorful and tasty.

Mustard and garlic roasted beef tenderloin with watercress

Serves 8

This is best prepared the day before and served chilled.

INGREDIENTS

½ cup extra virgin olive oil

4 garlic cloves, finely chopped

4 tbsp Dijon mustard

2 tbsp fresh rosemary

cracked black pepper

1 good-sized beef tenderloin, well trimmed

watercress, to serve

PREPARATION

Preheat oven to 425°F.

Combine 2 tablespoons of the oil with the garlic, mustard, rosemary, and some cracked black pepper. Add the beef tenderloin, coat in the mixture, cover and refrigerate for 2 hours.

In a large cast-iron skillet, heat the remaining oil on high, sprinkle the tenderloin with sea salt, then sear on all sides until brown. Put into the oven and cook to your desired degree of doneness. Allow to cool to room temperature, then refrigerate.

Serve at your picnic location with watercress and extra mustard.

Seared pork and eggplant panini

INGREDIENTS

¾ cup extra virgin olive oil

1 large eggplant, sliced into ⅛ inch pieces

2 tbsp apple cider vinegar

1 tbsp chopped garden chives

1 tbsp chopped parsley

1 tbsp chopped basil

1 garlic clove, finely chopped

2 large pork tenderloins, sliced ½ inch thick on the diagonal, pounded out

12 slices of Italian ciabatta bread, cut ¼ inch thick

12 slices of fontina cheese, large enough to cover the bread slices

butter

PREPARATION

In a large cast-iron pan, heat 4 tablespoons of the olive oil and add the eggplant slices. Fry over medium heat until golden brown on each side. Remove and drain on paper towels. Season with sea salt and pepper.

Mix together the vinegar, chives, parsley, basil, and garlic with 1 tablespoon of the olive oil. Pour over the eggplant slices and allow to stand at room temperature.

In a large cast-iron pan, heat 2 tablespoons of the oil, season the pork and fry over high heat until golden brown, about 1 minute per side. Keep warm.

Lay six slices of bread on a work surface and cover each evenly with the pork and the eggplant. Top with cheese. Place the remaining slices of bread on top and butter both sides on the outside.

Heat a cast-iron pan. Place three sandwiches in the pan and weigh down with a second pan, cooking for 3 minutes on each side or until golden brown and crispy all over. Repeat with the remaining sandwiches. Take to the beach and enjoy with a good bottle of wine.

Serves 6

Prepare just before packing up for your picnic, and wrap well to keep warm.

An Encounter

Macaroni Beach at sundown is my favorite swim in Mustique. I drive there in a little car with no more than a towel and my swimsuit, when all the sun-worshippers have returned to their villas and the beach is deserted. Driving back one evening around dusk, I met four French visitors at the crossroads. They were trying to get back to their yacht on the other side of the island, and needed a ride to the jetty, so I drove and deposited them, getting out to open the door and say goodbye.

To my outstretched hand, they offered a tip. "Non merci," I said. "I am the Prime Minister."

One lady said she was from the Ministry of Finance in Paris, and continued to press the tip on me.

"I know your President Chirac," I said. That really got them puzzled. How could this barefoot driver know their President?

Sir James Mitchell

Prime Minister Sir James Mitchell was the Member of Parliament representing Mustique and the Grenadines constituency for 35 years. His autobiography *Beyond the Islands* has recently been published by Macmillan Caribbean.

Toasted baguettes with oven-roasted tomatoes, garlic, and basil

Serves 8

Picnics are casual, relaxing, fun – and yes, somehow the food just tastes better outdoors. Spoon the tomato onto the toasted baguettes only when you're ready to indulge, this way they stay crunchy.

INGREDIENTS

24 plum tomatoes

1 tsp sugar

4 garlic cloves, cut into fine slivers

2 tbsp olive oil

2 tbsp balsamic vinegar

6 basil leaves, torn

24 slices of toasted baguette, prepared and kept in an airtight container

PREPARATION

Preheat oven to 400°F.

Halve the tomatoes crossways and arrange on baking trays. Put a small sprinkling of sugar and sea salt on each half, add the slivered garlic and drizzle with olive oil. Roast for 20 minutes. Reduce the oven to 300°F and roast for another 10 minutes. At this point, they should be starting to brown and have collapsed.

Remove from the oven and place in an airtight container. Sprinkle with the balsamic vinegar and basil leaves and cover. They should still be warm when you're ready to spoon them onto your bruschetta or toasts.

Leek, onion, and cheese tart

Serves 6–8

INGREDIENTS

Pastry:

1 cup all-purpose white flour

pinch of sea salt

¼ cup butter

¼ cup white vegetable fat (Crisco)

4 tbsp cold water

Filling:

2 tbsp butter

1½ cups sliced onions

¾ cup sliced leeks

4 eggs

1 cup cream

a small sprinkling of cayenne pepper

2 tbsp grated Gruyère cheese

PREPARATION

For the pastry, sift the flour and sea salt into a mixing bowl. Cut the butter and vegetable fat into small cubes. Add to the flour and mix together with your fingers until the mixture is well combined. Add the cold water and mix into a firm but pliable dough. Knead on a floured surface until smooth. Wrap in plastic wrap and chill for 30 minutes.

Preheat oven to 400°F.

For the filling, melt the butter in a skillet, then gently cook the onions and leeks over low heat for about 12 minutes. When cooked, drain well and set aside.

Roll out the chilled pastry dough on a floured surface until large enough to fit a 9 inch round loose-bottomed flan pan. Line the pan and trim the excess dough. Place a sheet of foil over the pastry then fill with baking beans and bake for 10 minutes. While baking, beat together the eggs, cream, cayenne, and sea salt and pepper to taste.

When pastry is partially cooked, remove the foil and baking beans and reduce oven temperature to 350°F. Arrange the onions and leeks in the pastry case and pour the egg mixture over. Sprinkle the Gruyère on top and return to the oven for an additional 30 minutes or until the pastry is golden brown.

Deliciously crisp, this light pastry with sweet-tasting onions and leeks is complemented by a creamy Gruyère filling. This is an ideal candidate for a perfect portable feast. Serve warm with a fresh green salad and some crusty bread.

Kevin's Caribbean fried chicken

Serves 8

The combination of citrus, mustard, and herbs is one of my favorites, with, of course, the addition of hot sauce.

INGREDIENTS

2 frying chickens, cut into 8 pieces

4 cups flour

peanut oil for frying

1 cup butter

Marinade:

½ cup orange juice

¼ cup lemon juice

1 tsp Dijon mustard

1 tbsp hot sauce

¼ cup peanut oil

3 garlic cloves, finely chopped

3 tbsp chopped parsley

3 tbsp chopped oregano

PREPARATION

Combine all of the marinade ingredients together. Mix thoroughly with the chicken pieces and season with sea salt and freshly cracked pepper. Allow to marinate for 45 minutes.

Drain the chicken pieces and dredge in the flour to coat fully. Heat the oil in a skillet on high. When it starts to smoke, turn to medium heat, add the butter and begin frying the chicken. Cook for 15–20 minutes until golden brown and crispy. You may take to your picnic warm or allow to cool. Serve with your favorite chutney.

Mango Caribbean champagne

INGREDIENTS
¼ cup light Caribbean rum
½ cup mango liqueur
1 dash of orange bitters
1½ cups champagne
4 slices fresh mango

PREPARATION
Combine the rum, mango liqueur, and bitters together. Keep in a small container to carry to the picnic. When at your location, divide equally between four chilled champagne glasses and top up with champagne. Stir gently and add the mango slices to garnish.

Serves 4

Those bubbles set a wonderful mood to commence a memorable picnic.

Spiced iced tea

INGREDIENTS
6 tsp black tea
3 whole cloves
2 whole cardamom pods, cracked
1 small cinnamon stick
1 tbsp honey
6 cups boiling water
1 cup warmed milk

PREPARATION
Place the black tea, cloves, cardamom, cinnamon, and honey in a pot. Add the boiling water and allow to steep for 5 minutes. Add the warmed milk and stir. Strain and chill. Serve with ice.

Serves 8

This cool spicy tea is perfect for those hot Caribbean days.

Taste the Sweetness

CHAPTER NINE
Taste the Sweetness: Island Desserts

Candy-coated anything can be good in moderation! And, of course, we are so blessed in these waters with such an abundance of tropical fruits like papaya, mango, sour sop, passion fruit, and bananas. Mix it all up with exotic spices like cloves, cinnamon, star anise, and nutmeg to enhance flavors and to push one's boundaries into discovering and creating new tastes. After all, most of us seem to have a weakness for something sweet – even after a full meal – so I've included a wonderful cross-section of Caribbean flavors in which to indulge.

Recipes

Hibiscus flower and honey ice cream | Candied ginger ice cream | Mango sorbet

Mustique's super-famous, super-rich caramel brownies

Trio of silky custards: passion fruit, coconut, and roasted banana crème brûlées | Banana fritters with rum sauce

Frozen lime and white chocolate torte with coconut crust | Spiced tropical fruit salad

Caramelized pineapple with cinnamon cream

Hibiscus flower and honey ice cream

INGREDIENTS
1 cup milk

3 cups whipping cream

½ cup honey

2 tbsp sugar syrup

½ cup dried hibiscus flowers (can be found at natural food store)

6 egg yolks, beaten

PREPARATION
In a heavy-bottomed saucepan over medium heat, heat the milk, cream, honey, and sugar syrup to simmering point. Pour over the dried hibiscus petals. Allow to steep for 20 minutes, then strain. Slowly pour over the eggs, whisking briskly until the mixture slightly thickens. Leave to cool and strain.

Freeze in an ice-cream maker following the manufacturer's directions.

NOTE
For added color and flavor, add some fresh hibiscus petals while the mixture is still warm.

Serves 6

The delicate flavor these gorgeous flowers impart enhances the natural sweetness of honey... simply sublime.

Candied ginger ice cream

Serves 6

Spicy and refreshing.

INGREDIENTS

4 egg yolks

5 tbsp white sugar

1½ cups whipping cream

½ cup whole milk

1 vanilla pod

½ tsp powdered ginger

3 tbsp chopped preserved ginger

PREPARATION

In a large bowl, whisk together the egg yolks and sugar. In a separate saucepan, heat together the whipping cream, milk, vanilla pod, and powdered ginger. Bring to a boil. Remove the vanilla pod and pour slowly into the egg mixture, briskly whisking the entire time.

Return the mixture to the saucepan on medium heat and stir until the mixture thickens enough to coat the back of a spoon without sliding off. Remove from heat, strain, add the preserved ginger and allow to cool.

Put into an ice-cream machine and churn according to the manufacturer's directions.

Mango sorbet

INGREDIENTS

1½ cups sugar

3 cups water

3 large ripe mangoes, seed removed and cut into slices

1 cup freshly squeezed orange juice

¼ cup Grand Marnier

PREPARATION

Heat the sugar and water until the sugar dissolves; set aside to cool.

In a food processor fitted with a metal blade, puree the mango to a pulp and add the orange juice. Stir into the cooled syrup and add the Grand Marnier. Pour into an ice-cream maker and churn according to the manufacturer's directions.

Serves 6

Always refreshing on a hot Caribbean day.

Mustique's super-famous, super-rich caramel brownies

INGREDIENTS
14 oz caramels

1 small can of evaporated milk

1 box of German Chocolate cake mix

¾ cup melted butter

1½ cups chopped nuts

1 small bag of chocolate chips, or about 8 oz

PREPARATION
Preheat oven to 350°F.

Melt the caramels with half the evaporated milk on low heat.

In a medium-sized bowl, mix the cake mix with the butter, nuts, and remaining milk (the batter will be thick in consistency). Spread half the batter in a buttered and floured 9 x 13 inch pan, making sure that the batter is spread about ¼ inch up the sides of the pan. Bake for 10 minutes and remove from oven.

Spread the melted caramel mixture and chocolate chips over the baked brownie mixture, making sure to keep the caramel away from the edges of the pan. Spread the remaining cake mixture on top using your fingers, pushing the batter to cover as much as possible – almost a marbled effect.

Bake for 18 minutes in the middle of the oven. Let cool completely before cutting into small squares – they're rich!

CHEF'S NOTE
These are the best gooey mess I've ever had!

Makes 12

Long-time Mustique resident Lorie Penniman has never given out this recipe before, despite dozens of requests over the years. Whether it's a holiday party, a beach picnic, or an after-dinner indulgence, these delights are sure to be enjoyed by all!

Trio of silky custards: passion fruit, coconut, and roasted banana crème brûlées

Serves 12

It just so happens this dessert is my favorite. For the different flavors I've created or adapted in this trio, I've used the distinct and popular Caribbean tropical fruits. These are all creamy and satisfying.

Passion fruit crème brûlée

INGREDIENTS

6 fresh passion fruit

2 tbsp water

10 large egg yolks

4 cups whipping cream

1 cup white sugar plus 12 tsp for sprinkling

1 tsp pure vanilla

PREPARATION

Preheat oven to 350°F.

Halve the passion fruits and scoop out the flesh with the seeds. Heat in a saucepan with the water. Strain, extracting as much juice as possible, and set aside. Beat the egg yolks in a large stainless-steel bowl.

In a heavy-bottomed pan, over medium heat, heat the whipping cream, sugar, passion juice, and vanilla. Stirring constantly, bring to a gentle simmer. Pour over the egg yolks slowly, whisking briskly as you pour. Strain through a fine sieve.

Place 12 ramekins in a large baking dish. Pour enough hot water into the dish to reach halfway up the sides of the ramekins. Evenly fill the ramekins with the passion fruit mixture. Bake in the middle of the oven for 35–40 minutes or until set in the center. Remove from oven and chill for at least 3 hours.

Sprinkle with white sugar and heat with a kitchen torch until the sugar is caramelized. Serve and enjoy.

Roasted banana crème brûlée

Serves 12

INGREDIENTS

4 ripe bananas

2 tbsp melted butter

10 large egg yolks

½ cup dark rum (optional)

4 cups whipping cream

1 tsp pure vanilla

½ tsp grated nutmeg

½ tsp ground cinnamon

1 cup brown sugar

12 tsp white sugar

PREPARATION

Preheat oven to 350°F.

To roast bananas, place them on a baking sheet and brush with the melted butter. Bake in the oven for 30–35 minutes. Remove, mash thoroughly and set aside. Beat the egg yolks in a large stainless-steel bowl. Heat the rum, if desired, until reduced by a quarter.

In a heavy-bottomed pan over medium heat, heat the whipping cream, vanilla, nutmeg, cinnamon, and brown sugar and, stirring constantly, bring to a gentle simmer. Pour over the egg yolks slowly, whisking briskly as you pour. Strain through a fine sieve and whisk in the mashed bananas and rum.

Place 12 ramekins in a large baking dish. Pour enough hot water into the dish to reach halfway up the sides of the ramekins. Evenly fill the ramekins with the banana mixture. Bake in the middle of the oven for 35–40 minutes or until set in the center. Remove from oven and chill for at least 3 hours.

Sprinkle with the white sugar and heat with a kitchen torch until the sugar is caramelized. Serve immediately.

Coconut crème brûlée

Serves 12

INGREDIENTS

2 cups pure coconut milk

½ cup Malibu rum

10 large egg yolks

4 cups whipping cream

1 cup condensed milk

1 tsp pure vanilla

5 tbsp grated fresh coconut

12 tsp white sugar

PREPARATION

Preheat oven to 350°F.

In a heavy-bottomed pan over medium heat, reduce the coconut milk and Malibu rum by a fifth. Set aside. Beat the egg yolks in a large stainless-steel bowl.

Heat the whipping cream, condensed milk, and vanilla, stirring constantly until it reaches a gentle simmer. Pour over the egg yolks slowly, whisking briskly as you pour. Strain through a fine sieve. Add the coconut rum mixture and the fresh coconut.

Place 12 ramekins in a large baking dish. Pour enough hot water into the dish to reach halfway up the sides of the ramekins. Evenly fill the ramekins with the coconut mixture. Bake in the middle of the oven for 40–45 minutes or until set in the center. Remove from oven and chill for at least 3 hours.

Sprinkle with the white sugar and heat with a kitchen torch until the sugar is caramelized. Serve immediately.

The Flavor of Mustique

The sand, cool air – tranquility
Majestic villas standing royally
The fisherman's shout, the smell of fish
The most pristine views that one could wish
Bare feet, bare back, bare bother, bare all!
Unfettered, nature is your mystic call.
The smells of oh-so tantalizing fare is hooking
From every house magic chefs are looking
And brewing and doing tropic-sweet delicious cooking
To bring heaven closer to the earth
To fill their guests and bring them mirth

On New Year's Eve, the yachts they come
Splendid flotilla, classic, painted golden
Nestled in the westering sun
Busy hub-bub fills the docks
Expectant throngs procure their stocks
The air is live with loving jive
Beach Bar at 12.00 is the "Party Hive."
Warm smiles and contentment hang around
Aiming to entrap – each one to bound
A magical land of fantasy
Where music is but idle breeze
And the crashing sound of misty sea
Dancers move in rhythmic cadence
Lovers love and give sweet fragrance
And birds fly high to survey with favor.
If you blend all these – then that's the flavor!

Cubby
Frank Roberts
February 2005

Banana fritters with rum sauce

INGREDIENTS

8 bananas, cut into thick angled slices

8 tbsp dark rum

2¼ cups unbleached white flour

1 tsp baking powder

pinch of sea salt

2 fresh eggs

2 cups cold water

2 cups canola oil

icing sugar for dusting

Sauce:

⅔ cup soft brown sugar

1 tsp ground cinnamon

1 tsp grated nutmeg

8 tbsp unsalted butter

6 tbsp banana liqueur

8 tbsp dark rum

PREPARATION

For the sauce, mix together the sugar, cinnamon, and nutmeg in a bowl. Melt the butter in a heavy pan. Add the sugar mix, banana liqueur, and dark rum and stir over medium heat until syrupy.

Toss the sliced bananas gently with the rum. Combine 2 cups flour with the baking powder and sea salt. Whisk in the eggs and cold water to make a smooth batter.

Heat the oil to about 350°F. Dust the banana slices with the balance of the flour. Dip into the batter mixture, shake and carefully lift out. Place the fritters in the hot oil and cook for 2 minutes on each side until golden brown. Remove and drain on paper towels.

Serve with the sauce, a dusting of icing sugar, and a generous helping of vanilla ice cream if desired.

Serves 8

Bananas contain three natural sugars: sucrose, fructose, and glucose. Combined with fiber, they give us an instant and sustained boost of energy. These delicious fritters are complemented when served with some creamy rich vanilla ice cream.

Frozen lime and white chocolate torte with coconut crust

Serves 8

This recipe focuses on the tart and distinctively aromatic lime. In hot climates, it refreshes one's mouth like no other citrus. The white chocolate is used as an accent for the lime and also complements the coconut crust.

INGREDIENTS

Crust:
8 tbsp unsalted butter
½ cup brown sugar
2½ cups unsweetened shredded coconut
1½ cups finely chopped almonds

Filling:
1½ cups white sugar
¾ cup milk
4 oz white chocolate
1 cup fresh lime juice
1 tbsp grated lime zest
8 egg yolks, beaten
4 cups whipping cream, whipped

PREPARATION

Preheat oven to 350°F.

For the crust, melt the butter with the sugar. Add the coconut and almonds until you have a "wet sand" texture. Press into a 9 inch spring-form pan and bake for 8 minutes. Allow to cool.

Meanwhile, heat the sugar and the milk in a stainless-steel pot. Add the white chocolate, lime juice and zest. When the chocolate has melted, whisk in the beaten egg yolks and continue to stir until the mixture slightly thickens. Cool this mixture over a bowl of ice and then fold in the whipped cream. Pour the mixture into the chilled pie crust. Freeze until ready to serve.

Spiced tropical fruit salad

INGREDIENTS

1½ cups tropical fruit juice

2 tbsp brown sugar

1 cinnamon stick

3 slivers fresh ginger, peeled

4 whole cloves

2 star anise

assortment of tropical fruits: mango, starfruit, cherry, papaya, pink grapefruit, passion fruit, sugar apple, banana

PREPARATION

Make the syrup by heating the fruit juice, brown sugar, and spices together. Allow to simmer for 5 minutes. Cool.

Prepare your chosen fruit by peeling and slicing into suitable-size pieces where appropriate. Add to the cooled syrup. Marinate for 1 hour before serving.

Serves 8

This awesome dessert gives us a distinct array of Caribbean fruits, with different textures accented by our island spices – and, of course, a sunburst of color.

Caramelized pineapple with cinnamon cream

Serves 6

Fragrant and totally pineappley.

INGREDIENTS

1 ripe pineapple, peeled and cored

¼ cup light brown sugar

8 tbsp unsalted butter

4 tbsp dark rum

1 cup whipping cream

4 tsp white sugar

1 tsp ground cinnamon

PREPARATION

Preheat oven to 350°F.

Slice the prepared pineapple crossways into six slices. Rub each slice with brown sugar. In a wide non-stick pan, heat the butter. When melted and sizzling, add the pineapple slices. On high heat, color each side. Transfer to a baking sheet, drizzle with the rum and bake in the oven for 10 minutes.

Meanwhile, whip the cream, white sugar, and cinnamon together.

Remove the caramelized pineapple slices from the oven. Place on a serving platter with any excess juice. Allow to cool slightly then serve with the whipped cinnamon cream.

Party at Kevin's

Happenings in Mustique aren't always dependent on who is on the island – but as it is said, "Fun begets fun." And on one special night, fun came delivered to us by a sailboat – with five Scandinavian girls on board to film a reality show. The "Pirate Girls," as they called themselves, were sailing through, with a several-day stop on Mustique.

Lucky us.

Kevin and I decided that we'd invite them over one evening – for a cooking demonstration of Caribbean delicacies and a cocktail party rolled into one. So the girls, plus their camera crew, director, and a few other guys working on the island showed up for what we knew would be an especially fun Mustique evening. A quick cooking presentation was followed by rounds of drinks and great music – which got louder with each song. We then moved to the pool table to play a hearty game of "Shot Pool," a regular game of eight ball, with the loser of the game downing a shot. That night, the drink of choice was apple sourpuss liqueur, and the party hit the high gears.

Faintly, over the din and coming from somewhere off near the bushes, we heard a faint "Help." At least we thought that's what we heard. No one moved, assuming it was the apple sourpuss speaking to us, or someone playing a joke. We then heard it again. And again. Someone dialed down the music, and we listened intently. Yes, it was still there. "Help" – this time a little louder, clearer. The panicked cry for help was coming from the pool's edge. Kevin, apparently, had forgotten to put the cover back on the top of his water tank – and standing there in a rather happy but panicked state, was a member of the film crew. (In Mustique, there is no fresh water, so all the houses have tanks where rainwater is gathered and stored.) The rescue effort must have taken a good 20 minutes, as we were all laughing so hard, we couldn't even muster the wherewithal to pull him out. Luckily the tank was only half-full and the poor bloke could actually stand.

The party quickly picked up where it left off – it was now nearly 5.00 a.m. As with most of Kevin's parties, it is always an exercise in "survival of the fittest." At that hour, it was three men left with four women.

Needless to say, the story must happily end here . . .as it is that what-happens-in-Kevin's-house-stays-in-Kevin's-house code of honor that I will always follow.

Richard Schaeffer

The Midnight Hour

CHAPTER TEN

The Midnight Hour:
Drinks and More for the Midnight Rendezvous

At the midnight hour, bodies sway under the palms, hands intertwine on a quiet sandy beach, the moon illuminates the silhouette of lovers frolicking, and the hammocks at Macaroni or Lagoon are otherwise dark

ten

and quiet. This is the moment to let your imagination go wild and flow, along with the cocktails and treats. Aphrodisiacs aside, let these recipes – and all that is around you – stimulate your senses.

Recipes

Champagne passion fruit cocktail | Mojito moonlight | Sex on the beach cocktail | A passionate kiss

Beachfire roasted marshmallows | Tropical fruit jellies | Chocolate-dipped candied ginger and orange peel

Champagne passion fruit cocktail

INGREDIENTS

4 oz passion fruit juice
4 oz cranberry juice
2 oz Grand Marnier
ice
generous topping of champagne

PREPARATION

Pour the juices and the Grand Marnier into a shaker with ice. Shake vigorously, and strain into chilled flutes. Top off with champagne. Cheers!

Serves 2

To enhance those passionate times alone with someone special... Impress with your bar tending skills – and don't forget the ice!

Mojito moonlight

INGREDIENTS

12 mint sprigs
8 tsp sugar
12 tbsp fresh lime juice
ice
6 oz light rum
club soda or seltzer
lemon slices

PREPARATION

Muddle half the mint with the sugar. Add the lime juice and stir thoroughly. Top with ice. Add rum and mix, and top off with chilled club soda or seltzer. Add a lemon slice and top off with the remaining mint.

Serves 4

Refreshing, cool, and minty.

Sex on the beach cocktail

Serves 2

The name says it all, doesn't it?

INGREDIENTS
4 oz vodka

3 oz peach schnapps

cranberry juice

grapefruit juice

PREPARATION
Add the vodka and peach schnapps to a highball glass. Fill with equal measures of cranberry juice and grapefruit juice, and stir.

A passionate kiss

Serves 2

Very sensual, totally indulgent. Embrace this moment.

INGREDIENTS
drop of Angostura bitters

1 sugar cube

4 oz champagne

splash of Campari

PREPARATION
Drop the Angostura bitters onto the sugar cube and place in a champagne glass. Add the champagne and a splash of Campari. Enjoy!

Beachfire roasted marshmallows

INGREDIENTS

1 bag of large marshmallows

PREPARATION

Start by digging a hole in a sheltered quiet corner, just deep enough to build a small fire. Prepare your fire with wood and coals and light, allowing it to burn until the coals are hot.

Push as many marshmallows as desired on the ends of sticks or bamboo skewers, making sure they are secure. Hold the marshmallows over the coals about 2 inches above the heat source, turning. Continue until the marshmallows turn your desired color. Remove from the fire. Allow the marshmallows to cool slightly.

Handling with care, remove each marshmallow one by one, feeding your partner first of course! Eat and enjoy – and most definitely get messy!

NOTE

Remember the Golden Rule: bury your ashes with sand when the evening is complete.

We are all kids at heart – just admit it. So, surprise that special someone with some midnight sticky fun on the beach that's bound to get you both laughing.

My First 24 Hours
on Mustique 34 Years Ago

My first night on Mustique was March 3, 1973. Food played a major role right from the start.

In a 1970s' issue of *Gourmet Magazine*, I had seen a two-page aerial photograph of L'Ansecoy Bay, pristine and undeveloped, and had read that the island was wild and unspoiled but had civilized accommodations and good food. It was late afternoon on March 3 when my husband and I and my friends Neal and Gail Curtin arrived from Boston and were greeted by Colin Tennant at the Cotton House where we were staying. Colin announced with enthusiasm, "Great news. There is a party for Princess Margaret tonight and you are all invited. It is a costume party with an Arab theme."

"Oh good," my six-foot-five, 290-pound friend and fellow lawyer said. "I just happen to have brought three of my favorite costumes." When Colin realized that Neal did not, in fact, have any costume and was not intending to wear one, he said, "Oh no, no, my boy. We shall get a costume for you." One of the only double sheets on the island was made into a toga, and a wreath of leaves was made for his head.

Then I said that I was really very tired and would rather just have a quiet dinner at the hotel. "Unfortunately," said Colin, "all the staff will be doing the party, so if you wish to have dinner, you will have to attend the party."

The party then began at 8 p.m. at Oceanus, which was Arne's first house, and lasted until 3.30 a.m. Everyone on the island – about 40 people – was there in costume. Men from the village, holding four-foot fire torches lined the steep driveway for light. There were at least five imported musical groups, much drink, and many courses. My British husband was seated next to Princess Margaret at the head of the table with Colin, and I was seated at the far end of the table with the other Americans. Basil, who later became the legendary owner of Basil's Bar, sat next to me at the very bottom.

Near the end of the party, guests began to jump in the swimming pool and Neal was rewarded with the sight of the beautiful Gala Mitchell, who was there as Salome in seven veils (scarves), swimming in the veils, which became more transparent when wet.

The next morning at the Cotton House, we awoke to see the SS *Antilles*, the second largest ship of the French Line, motionless in L'Ansecoy Bay, still embedded in the coral reef where it had run aground in 1971. It has long ago succumbed to time and tide, and has disappeared.

But I have returned every year since.

Margaret Douglas-Hamilton

A few years back,
I had the privilege
of working at the
Moulin de Mougin,
under world-
renowned, three-
star chef Roger
Verge. During
my time there, I
learned the perfect
formula for these
wonderful jellies.

Tropical fruit jellies

INGREDIENTS

Please use this as a guideline, but of course with a little trial and error they should become a perfect treat just for you!

Fruit	Pulp (puree)	Sugar	Pectin	Cooking time (once boiled)
citrus or passion fruit	4 cups (3–4 lb fruit)	4 ⅔ cups	5 tbsp + 1 tsp	8 minutes
mangoes or peaches	4 cups (2¼ lb fruit)	4 ⅔ cups	5 tbsp	10 minutes
red fruits	4 cups (2¼ lb fruit)	4½ cups	4 tbsp + 2 tsp	5–8 minutes

PREPARATION

First, select your desired ripened fruit and prepare for making the jellies. Wash, peel, stem, pit or seed the fruit you have picked. In a food processor or blender, blend the fruit into a fine puree.

In a non-reactive saucepan, combine the puree with nine tenths of the sugar and bring to a boil, whisking constantly.

In a bowl, combine the remaining sugar and the pectin. Add this mixture to the saucepan and continue to cook, whisking constantly for the given time, allowing it to reach about 220–230°F on a candy thermometer.

Pour the mixture immediately onto a baking sheet lined with parchment paper, and spread to about ⅓ inch thickness. Let cool completely.

After cooling, cut out candies into suitable-sized squares. Finally, roll the pieces in sugar and let dry for 2–3 hours.

Store in a sealed container, separating each layer with a piece of wax paper to avoid sticking.

Chocolate-dipped candied ginger and orange peel

INGREDIENTS
2 oz semi-sweet chocolate

2 tbsp unsalted butter

1 tbsp Cointreau (orange liqueur)

8 oz crystallized ginger pieces

4 oz candied orange peel pieces

PREPARATION
Melt the chocolate in a double boiler, making sure not to let the water boil. When the chocolate has melted, add the butter, remove from heat and stir in the orange liqueur. While warm, dip the ginger and orange pieces into the chocolate, so that they are three-quarters coated. Place on waxed paper and refrigerate for at least 1 hour or until firm. Take with you to your midnight rendezvous... brownie points for sure!

Such an interesting taste treat with the flavor of orange and ginger together – definitely decadent!

Mustique Profiles

The Firefly

The Firefly was built as a private villa by Arne Hasselqvist, who built all of the earlier houses on the island, including Mick Jagger's Stargroves, David Bowie's Britannia Bay (now Felix Dennis's Mandalay), and Princess Margaret's Les Jolies Eaux – to name but a few. Firefly was commissioned by a Texas lady, Billy Mitchell, who sailed into Britannia Bay in the late sixties to be greeted by Lord Colin Glenconner waving his cane and white hat. She promptly decided to buy the lot on the hill overlooking the bay so that she could shout instructions to her crew from the veranda. She named it the Firefly because the trees surrounding the house are lit up at night by hundreds of fireflies year round.

In the eighties, with the increasing costs of living on the island, Billy decided to run a "bed and breakfast" at the Firefly to help defray expenses. She did this until 1994, with the help of two staff (a cook/maid and a handyman), and offering a continental breakfast. She then decided to sell the Firefly and advertised it in a Caribbean property newsletter.

Stan and Elizabeth Clayton, originally from England, were looking for a business in the Caribbean so that they could live in their favorite part of the world. Prior to buying the Firefly they had lived in Grenada without a business, and despite being in one of the most beautiful areas in the world were slowly dying of boredom. When they saw the ad for the Firefly, Stan and Elizabeth knew it was the place for them, and bought it sight unseen, taking possession in 1995.

It was a daunting task to renovate the Firefly, which had fallen into a state of disrepair, mainly due to its proximity to the ocean. There was no paved road, no mains water, and single-phase electricity (which meant that if you switched on a toaster in the kitchen the lamps would dim in the lounge!). The "garden" consisted of an incline covered in a wilderness of bush and trees, so steep that if you climbed down, you couldn't get back up! The Claytons gutted the building over the years, room by room, completely remodeling the bedrooms, building private patios with plunge pools, replacing every piece of furniture and equipment in the house. They built staff quarters, a new kitchen, restaurant, and bar, but still retained the original charm and appeal of the house. They landscaped the steep hillside into a tropical garden with private patios and decks, built a beautiful swimming pool with a "disappearing edge," fed by a waterfall from a smaller pool that is also fed by a waterfall. A Jacuzzi was added in the grounds, surrounded by flamboyant bougainvillea and frangipani trees. Fish ponds, joined by a series of waterfalls, cascade down the slope next to the steps to the pool area.

Firefly now flourishes as an exclusive retreat, with eighteen staff looking after just eight guests. A stay there, as it is said, is truly an "Experience"!

Firefly, Bequie, coming soon. . .

The Cotton House

The Cotton House in Mustique sits at the very heart of the island – as the jewel in the Caribbean crown – representing all of the unique beauty, intimacy, and grace that is Mustique. Those fortunate enough to visit oftentimes never really leave, as the Cotton House creates flavors, feelings, and memories for its visitors unlike any other hotel – or any other place – anywhere else in the world.

Nestled around the white sand beach of Endeavor Bay, the Cotton House originally served as an 18th-century coral warehouse and sugar mill for the native Mustiquans. Historical photographs of the island feature this small stone windmill as its center – in some ways the island's architectural beacon. Additional images from the past four decades depict the slow evolution of Mustique's growth, with the mill and its surrounding buildings still at the center. Today, extensive and careful renovations to the original Cotton House structures, beautiful and creative plantings and landscaping, ponds and intricate stonework, and a world-class spa, tennis courts, and pool bring visitors to the island from all over the world.

The late British designer Oliver Messel and one of Mustique's pioneer builders, the late Arne Hasselqvist, built the Cotton House from the framework of these beautiful original stone structures, playing to the sea views, the topography, and its perfect beach.

The Cotton House underwent a full-scale renovation and expansion project in 2004, and today holds the distinction of being one of the "Leading Small Hotels of the World." It is widely recognized as one of the Caribbean's top established luxury resorts. Today, twenty distinctive rooms and suites create an intimate experience for every guest, and the new spa and fitness center provide a beachside escape for rejuvenation, beauty, and peace of mind.

It has been said that nothing happens unless first we dream. And for those who first stepped upon the wild and untamed beaches of Mustique so many years ago, who could have imagined the discovery that would lead to the dream that is the Cotton House as it is today?

Basil's

There will someday be a dictionary entry that will include the verb, to have been "Basil'd." And the definition is: to have experienced rapture while dancing under the stars; To have been victimized by rum punch; to have had the time of your life in a simple yet exclusive establishment on what is possibly one of the most deliciously exclusive islands in the world. The derivative would be, "to Basil," which is to have done any of these things in the company of Basil himself: to have been regaled by his stories (so famous they have been numbered by those closest to him); to have been the recipient of too many glasses of fine French wine; to have giggled and danced and eaten far too much good food at the "power table"; to have shared an evening with one who truly enjoys and celebrates life.

To be on Mustique at Basil's Bar . . .

Around the world, bars come and go. Some are formula creations of large restaurant conglomerates, others manifestations of the long-held dream of an ardent host, and others still, the naïve enterprise of someone who thinks the business is a license to print money. Few bars succeed, fewer still excel. The legion of legendary bars is small: Harry's Bar, the Oak Room, Rick's, the fictional Cheers, and Basil's.

Basil's Bar in Mustique is listed as one of the top bars in the world again and again. One reason is location of course, but it is something about the way guests' molecules begin to vibrate when they step onto the worn floorboards of the beach bar, with its odd-shaped booths, bamboo walls, and polished cement dance floor – surrounded by a jewel-blue sea. Perched on stilts over the sighing seas of Britannia Bay, Basil's commands a blue view of the twinkling ocean, ringside seats of a horizon ignited by vapors of orange at sunset, and starlit evenings kissed by the offshore breeze.

Often, Basil's Bar is noted because of its celebrity clientele. The famous, powerful and talented find solace in anonymity as their molecules also gently vibrate – compelling guests to relax and enjoy the libations of the bar. Popular and unusual drinks like Hurricane David (said to blow you off your bar stool) and Basil's Rum Punch (as smooth as it is incapacitating) lubricate and liberate patrons. The food at Basil's is worth the trip even for the blasé: Basil's burger and fries, chicken satay, and garlic shrimp are addictive. Evenings, the dinner crowd dines on lobster (the hands-down specialty of the house), local fish, sumptuous steaks, and, of course, the Wednesday Night Jump Up BBQ featuring roasted pig.

2005 recipient of the OBE (Order of the British Empire), for his notable and honorable work in supporting the children of Mustique through the Basil Charles Educational Foundation, Basil is known for his giving and charity. At just over six feet – always dressed in bright shirts or colorful kaftans – he is a formidable party animal, as serious about having fun as he is about business, and often at the bar erupting in joyful laughter as he victimizes friends, both old and newly made.

This is not a mythical place: Basil's Bar and Mustique are as real as rain and as nourishing too. There are many things in life we long to do, things we want to become, things we hope to experience. Sadly, the meaningful things on our list are often unattainable, and others just don't live up to the hype. Basil's Bar is an exception: allow yourself to be Basil'd and fall into the hedonistic playful spirit inside you. Let the inspiration of an adult's happy laughter take you there – to Basil's Bar and to Mustique.

About the Contributors

Elizabeth Penniman has a rich heritage in Mustique, having first come to the island nearly 20 years ago with her father and stepmother, long-time Mustique residents Russell and Lorie Penniman. She is a published author and writer, having spent years in the White House, Executive Branch, and publishing fields. Elizabeth is the president of Pen & Ink Consulting, traveling worldwide for private and corporate clients to develop executive communications strategies. Today, Elizabeth and her three children enjoy Mustique more than any other place in the world.

Sophie Munro is a freelance photographer and writer specializing in travel and interiors. She contributes to numerous publications and travels worldwide on commissions. English by birth, Sophie now resides in New York. *A Taste of Mustique* is her first book.

Acknowledgments

The effort to create *A Taste of Mustique* has been a labor of love by a great number of people who love the beauty and simplicity of Mustique, its food, and the people who live and visit here as much as we do.

We'd like to thank the many people who gave us their stories and poems, their recipes, their counsel, and their support. It is not possible to name them all, but their contributions have helped us to bring the real tastes of Mustique to life.

We'd like to thank Brian Alexander, managing director of the Mustique Company, who gave us his blessing early on in our work.

And Felix Dennis, who has been a wonderful source of invaluable advice and friendship to our crew from the very beginning.

Joe Hodanich took our words, ideas, recipes, and photography and blended them with his wonderful touch for design to create something truly beautiful on every one of these pages.

To Charlotte Martin, who worked diligently to make sense of hundreds of recipes and even more pages of text, patiently editing, correcting, measuring, translating, and otherwise keeping us honest…and laughing.

And finally, to the people of Mustique, who we all will forever keep in our memories and hearts. Thank you for sharing this special place with us – always with graciousness, kindness, and hospitality.

Food Index

A

ackra 130
almonds 50, 110, 124
Amaretto 114, 117
anchovies 88
apples 5, 54, 84, 166
Angostura bitters 41, 175
artichokes 85
arugula leaves 82, 121
avocados 55, 65, 118

B

bacon 11, 33, 88, 128
baguettes 145
bananas 4, 20, 94, 114, 160, 164, 166
basil 85, 145
beef 48, 78, 136, 139
bran 4
brandy 84
breadfruits 33, 40
breads 4–5, 20, 83
Brie cheese 87
broccoli 138
broths 76, 97, 110
    see also soups
brownies 156

C

cabbage 137
Caesar salad 88
cakes 16, 23, 24, 156
callaloo 94
Campari 175
candied orange peel 182
caper berries 87
carambolas (starfruit) 34, 166
caramels 156
carrots 5, 39, 50, 70, 77, 94, 103, 109, 120, 137
cashew nuts 78
cauliflower 138
celery 33, 50, 70, 76, 77, 98, 104, 110, 120

champagne 148, 174, 175
chayote 98
cheese 32, 85, 87, 88, 103, 122, 140, 146
cherries 166
chicken 34, 36, 80, 97, 131, 136, 147
chickpeas 122
chili peppers 50, 78, 97
chives 71, 98
chocolate 21, 156, 165, 182
chorizo sausages 80
christophenes 32, 60, 98
ciabatta bread 140
cilantro 62, 65, 66, 76, 78, 97, 120
cinnamon 4, 5, 6, 8, 12, 16, 24
citrus fruits 181
    see also lemons; oranges
cloves 12, 26
cocktails 114, 116, 117, 148, 174, 175
coconut 5, 20, 24, 54, 60, 109, 132, 161, 165
coconut cream 114, 117
coconut milk 39, 76, 97, 109, 110, 131, 161
coconut water 60, 76
Cointreau 182
conch 70
cookies 18, 21
crab cakes 66
crabs 56, 66
cranberry juice 116, 117, 174, 175
cream 8, 98, 103, 104, 152, 159, 168
cream cheese 122
crème brûlées 159–61
crystallized ginger 182
cucumbers 42, 77, 103, 109
custards 159

D

dates 4, 159
desserts 152–4, 156, 159, 164, 165, 181
dill 109
dips 122
dough, for roti 136
dried fruit 3, 5
drinks 2, 12, 26, 28, 41, 84, 114, 116, 117, 148,
    174, 175

E

eddoes 94
eggplant 122, 140
eggs 152, 159, 160, 164, 165
evaporated milk 156

F

fennel 58
feta cheese 122
figs 128
fish 55, 57, 58, 60, 64, 65, 72, 88, 94
five-fingers (carambolas) 34, 166
focaccia bread 83
French toast 8
fritters 70, 164
fruit juices
    see cranberry juice; lemon juice; lime juice; orange
    juice; passion fruit juice; pineapple juice; tropical
    fruit juice
fruit salad 166

G

galanga 77
ginger 6, 12, 18, 26, 28, 36, 50, 62, 64, 76, 77, 97,
    153, 182
Grand Marnier 154, 174
granola 3
grapefruit juice 175
green beans 72
green onions 60, 78, 94, 97, 130
green seasoning 70
grenadine syrup 114, 117
grouper fish 57, 60

Gruyère cheese 146
guacamole 118
guava jelly 24, 25

H

hazelnuts 124
hibiscus 42, 116, 152
honey 2, 3, 34, 87, 131
hot peppers 39, 44, 55, 60, 94, 130

I

ice cream 152, 153

J

jellies 181
jerk seasoning 44, 47

L

lamb 47
leeks 145
lemon grass 76, 77, 78, 97
lemon juice 10, 23, 88, 103, 109, 122, 147
lemons 16, 23, 36, 84
lentil cakes 120
lentils 97, 120
lettuce 42, 88
lime juice 2, 26, 34, 41, 44, 54, 57, 58, 62, 65, 76,
    78, 84, 94, 97, 109, 117, 118, 131, 137, 165, 174
limes 26, 55, 72, 97
lobsters 60, 104

M

Malibu 116, 117, 161
mango chutney 67
mango liqueur 148
mango preserve 6
mangoes 2, 6, 16, 28, 50, 62, 67, 117, 148, 154,
    166, 181
marinated dishes 77, 124
marshmallows 176
milk 2, 4, 8, 76
mint 109, 122, 174
molasses 10, 18, 20
Mozzarella cheese 85

People and Places Index